*Praise* ...

Phill Bragg's *Needle, Ball, and Alcohol* has me itching to take the front seat of his antique biplane—provided he is flying of course! He beautifully captures his passion for his vintage World War II trainer, the people he encounters, and the adventure of travel with a curious nature, a love of history, and a self-deprecating sense of humor that keeps the reader turning pages. Such an interesting, fun read!

**Becky S. Ramsey**

Author of *French By Heart: An American Family's Adventures in La Belle France.*

Phill Bragg's book, *Needle, Ball, and Alcohol*, takes you on a cross-country trip in an old open-cockpit biplane. As you read you'll experience the trip as if you are along in the front cockpit. He writes down all the right things to make you love the journey—the seeing rivers and roads, the smelling trees and earth, the feel of smooth morning air. You will understand what flying was like when it required not a computer, but a pilot's eyes, ears, and soul. Bragg knows how to make you feel the exhilaration of it all. And he loves his old, beautiful aircraft almost as much as he loves his mama.

**Clyde Edgerton**

Author of *The Floatplane Notebooks* and *Solo, My Adventures in the Air*

# NEEDLE, BALL, & ALCOHOL

### The Second Great Fleet Biplane Excursion

# PHILL BRAGG

Needle, Ball, & Alcohol

Published by
Clouds I've Known Publishing Co.
www.cloudsiveknownpublishing.com

ISBN:  978-0-9906863-0-9

Printed in the United States of America
Mira Digital Publishing
Chesterfield, MO 63005

To my wife,
without whom I would never
have owned
an old biplane.

*To Yoshi,*
*Nice meeting*
*you.*
*Enjoy!*
*Phil*

v

# CHAPTER ONE

A THREE-TERM SHERIFF UP in Franklin County once told me that banjos have souls; he had shown me the way of the claw hammer banjo and he said banjos were special, not like guitars or even fiddles. After flying airplanes for more than thirty years, I know that airplanes have souls too. They are not like cars or boats; they are ever so special. But especially the old ones.

When I was twenty years old and a very inexperienced pilot, I read of a place east of Wichita where you could land on grass and taxi on the public street to an old hotel and eat lunch. I told myself I would go there and that I would do it only in an open-cockpit biplane. Thirty-four years later I bought a 1941 Fleet Model 16B, restored lovingly over a decade by an old-school aeronautical engineer from the days of slide rules and giant drafting tables.

He sold it to me, a complete stranger, because a mutual friend had told him I wanted to fly that airplane all across the United States. He did not want to see it only pulled out of a hangar on calm Sunday afternoons for a couple of circuits around the patch. He wanted that airplane to travel and to be seen and enjoyed by those who would know why to appreciate it. Sadly, he would not live to see pictures of the Fleet parked proudly beside a Rocky Mountain trout stream or on the Kansas prairie. But the Fleet would do those things and more.

This was not the Fleet's first adventure, but it was the one which finally took me to Beaumont, where I could taxi up to the old hotel. My friend, Wayland, went with me. He loves road trips and will endure any mode of travel and any of its inconveniences just to detour in order to see the world's largest acorn or the world's biggest hand-dug well. He is an intrepid traveler who believes in the journey as much as the destination. So, to be in my front cockpit was almost inconsequential to Wayland. If I had told him I was driving out to the Midwest on an old riding lawnmower, he would have been right there sitting on it somehow. For me though, it had to be in an antique, open-cockpit biplane. I believe in the journey as much as the destination too, but for me, seeing America from the rear seat of the Fleet is the destination. It is both. It is a dream I have dreamed since I was twenty years old reading about grass strips and the little mom-and-pop cafes that sat beside the airfields. Many of these establishments have disappeared during the three decades it took me to finally buy an old biplane, but some are still out there if you search for them.

Beyond Beaumont though was Greensburg, Kansas, which would be our westernmost point of landing and was originally the motivation for our excursion. We had met much of the town's population several years before under somewhat tragic circumstances and we wanted to return for a visit.

# CHAPTER TWO

OUR DEPARTURE WAS DELAYED for a whole year because I had to remove my center section fuel tank for a repair. The tank was easily fixed but the resulting fabric repair was huge and I am the slowest airplane mechanic in the world, especially when I am learning a new art. I was learning the mysterious ways of dope and fabric and the curve was a long, high one. But it was as much a part of the upcoming journey as any other aspect of the trip; it was showing the Fleet that I wanted to understand it and care for it. The shame of it was that my dad had tried to teach me these things when I was a teenager and he was busy keeping two Piper Pawnee crop dusters in the air. But I cared more about watching television after school than helping him replace cylinders or rib stitch out at the grass strip where he flew. No childhood was more wasted.

Better late than never though and there I was all last summer using his old EAA dope and fabric manuals, still in mint condition, trying to unravel the secrets of seine knots and why butyrate sticks to nitrate but not the other way around. By October—I said I was slow—the job was completed. My big fabric repair turned out okay and passed muster for the Fleet's annual inspection, but I was glad it was on the top wing and mostly out of sight. You never knew when one of those Oshkosh Grand Champion craftsmen was going to wander out of a hangar at some obscure little airport while you were pumping gas and take a really close look.

There was one other repair that had to be made as well. I had replaced a copper head gasket only twenty flying hours previously and it had ruptured again. I had landed after returning from Ball Field's thirty-ninth annual fly-in and immediately heard the steam-hissing sound coming from the number four cylinder. There was much more to be learned about this seemingly straightforward repair. Through Al Ball's (no relation to the Ball Field gang) generous giving of his encyclopedic knowledge of the Kinner engine, I learned that I must anneal the copper gasket with my torch, which made it pliable and better able to seal the space between cylinder head and barrel. There was also a procedure to properly break in the new gasket and re-torque the cylinder nuts once I flew the airplane again.

Howsoever cautious and wary I may be with needle and thread and nitrate dope, I am a thousand times more careful when I am working on an engine. My normal snail's pace is even slower than usual in order to avoid mistakes. I did not grow up disassembling and reassembling my toys like some kids. I watched television. And while that garnered me a certain kind of knowledge, it did not teach me to time magnetos or to weld aircraft tubing. But one habit I had somehow inherited from my dad was to read manuals and to do things pursuant to the manufacturer's instructions. He was a firm believer in that; he detested shade tree mechanics. *Jacklegs* he called them. Likewise, I had learned to defer to the expertise of people like Al Ball who, like my dad, were meticulous and precise.

Summer became autumn and then winter had arrived by the time I finished all the repairs, and so our trip would be delayed until the following spring or summer. Our exact departure date would depend on our work schedules. Wayland would be sure not to schedule any court cases that week and I would have to be without commitments to any of the companies for which I did contract flying. I had learned in recent years that talk is cheap and there is a finite number of days left for us to make dreams come true. Life is short; shorter for some than others. That is what Duvall's character had said in the greatest western ever made. I had decided a few years ago that since I could not ascertain when I would die, I would not squander any more of my precious time. I would not let the conventions of planning for retirement and social security prevent me from doing what had become so important, that is, living. I would not lie on my deathbed with any regrets. And I most certainly would not discontinue the Fleet's adventures across America for any reason.

# CHAPTER THREE

I GAVE WAYLAND AND his wife, Jane, their first open-cockpit biplane ride one beautiful fall afternoon at the grass strip where I live. They were enchanted, as most people are, by the experience and it was the genesis of our flight to the Midwest. The romance of old biplanes was not entirely lost on my friend and it was undoubtedly a conveyance he had never used on any of his previous road trips, some of which are near legendary. As the time drew closer, he became more and more excited about our undertaking and, of course, so did I.

In the weeks before our departure I stayed busy with the smaller, last-minute maintenance details which were no less important than the larger ones. I checked magneto timing and cleaned and gapped the spark plugs. I drained the engine oil and added fresh and pulled the Cuno screen to inspect it. I enjoy changing oil more than anything else; I feel I am administering a blood transfusion to the one hundred and sixty-horsepower Kinner. Engines must surely luxuriate in fresh oil. A happy engine has new, clean oil.

I greased and lubricated and inspected every airframe component that needed it. Cables, turnbuckles, oleos, and flying wires. I rejuvenated some dope that was showing early signs of cracking. I organized everything in the small baggage compartment behind the rear cockpit: first aid kit, engine oil, Marvel Mystery oil, chocks, tie-downs, rocker grease and grease gun, fuel stick, windscreen cleaner, rudder lock, tool bag, rags, extra spark plugs and a hand crank. I always ran out of volume before I ever exceeded the compartment's sixty-four pound weight restriction. The Fleet was made to teach cadets how to fly, not to go on cross-country jaunts with lots of camping gear. Those antique airplanes are called DeHavilland Beavers.

I can never sleep the night before a long-awaited flight, so I did not even try. After I thought every task had been completed, I pulled up a chair on the hangar floor beside the Fleet and began at the nose and visually inspected every part all the way to the tailwheel. Did I forget to inspect anything? Did I forget to service something? Do I have the tools I may need should this or that break? Especially the ones I have specially bent and shaped to make certain jobs easier. And don't forget the paperwork. Restored antique or not, the Fleet has a Standard Airworthiness Certificate and is a factory-built airplane as far as the FAA is concerned. Yep, it's all there, snug and secure. Wait. Where are the cockpit cover and the small tarp for the Kinner? Can't forget those since it's more than possible we may get caught out in the rain before we get back home. Bad enough if the Fleet gets soaking wet outdoors, but at least I can keep water off the engine and out of the two cockpits with those covers. And even without rain, I have found that cool mornings with lots of dew can condense water inside the magnetos. They never dry quickly either.

Unabashedly, I tell the Fleet I don't think I have forgotten anything and that I think we are ready for another adventure. I get out of my chair and walk over beside the fuselage and lean against it like a child would lean against a big family dog. I love this airplane; it is the only one I have ever owned and it is exactly what I have wanted since I was twenty years old and did not know much about flying.

My wife, Alice, and I bought the Fleet after we had been married more than a decade. She had known of my dream involving an open-cockpit biplane as long as she had known me. Even without my passion for flying, it still appealed to her because she had that kind of spirit. I could never have owned the Fleet without her in my life, but that is another story for another book.

I decided I had not overlooked anything and sat at the round wood table in the rear of my hangar to organize the new sectional charts which arrived in the mail the day before. I had ordered enough charts to accommodate most deviations we might make in our planned routes because of weather, or just due to getting lost, which was not beyond my capabilities.

# CHAPTER FOUR

THE MORNING I WAS to leave Todd's Cross was bright and sunny and a little windy. Even as the sun was rising above the tall pines which guard the east end of my runway, I could tell the day was going to be a scorcher, breezy or not. The First Great Fleet Excursion, which had taken me and Alice all the way to the Grand Canyon, was during a record-breaking heat wave across the South. So history was repeating itself, but that would be fine with me; it had been a magical flight with my wife.

In the morning, a friend helped me push the Fleet outside, past the big tin hangar doors and into the eastern North Carolina humidity. I swung the tail around and chocked the tires because the engine would require at least ten minutes of warming up, even when the temperature outside is eighty degrees. The Kinner engine is very cold-natured and the old manuals say not to exceed one hundred and twenty pounds of oil pressure during take-off, but that is nearly impossible in cold weather without actually preheating the oil before starting.

This morning though was warm and it would be possible to keep the oil pressure within limits. It made me wonder though how the Canadians operated this airplane in Nova Scotia during the war, all winter long in the snow and ice. I guess when there's a world war in progress you do what you must to defeat an enemy such as they faced. I know they used greenhouse canopies in the coldest weather, attached to rails on the fuselage, and they removed the wheels in order to attach skis for use on the snow. I had seen the old photos of those canopies and the skis in books, but none of those would be needed on this summer's flight.

It was time to start the Kinner engine and begin our trip. Starting that engine is one of my favorite things to do because it is satisfying on so many levels. After all, it is the source of the Fleet's ability to move about the sky with impunity. Well, actually it's a co-source since we have to count the wings. But the wings have no internal moving parts. My Kinner R-55 however has many moving metal parts and they are in many different shapes, all coming together in what, to me, never ceases to be less than a miracle. With no electric starter, it must be hand-propped, which is almost a taboo procedure in some circles. I believe it is because we have become too litigious and fearful of responsibility in our no-fault society. Oh, they give hand-propping seminars at the great Wisconsin fly-in, but the airplane being used for the demonstration is so well-secured to the Earth prior to starting you would think it might escape and devour small children. It looked like Gulliver's Lilliputians had got hold of it. I am just teasing of course, because I do admire their willingness to broach the subject at least.

I do not mean to belittle the carefulness and attention to detail required to safely hand-prop an airplane. It is a serious matter, but also the very epitome of the nostalgia and romance of fabric-covered biplanes and it gives us insight of the dashing men and women who flew them in the years between the world wars, which is my favorite era of aviation. So, for me, hand-propping is both an honorable ritual and a privilege which I never take for granted and of which I never tire.

Main wheels are chocked. Double-check that the magnetos are off and the fuel valve is on. Pull the thick wooden Sensenich prop through five blades. Now switch on the left magneto to employ its impulse coupling for sufficient starting voltage. Mixture full rich and throttle cracked for the correct amount of air the engine seems to like for starting. Carburetor heat off.

Now comes the really fulfilling part: walk around to the left side of the engine, straddle the main wheel, insert the big aluminum cranking handle through the access hole in the metal cowling. Stand on the tire and pump the primer handle four times. I glance in the front cockpit to double-check the throttle position. My dad once recovered a whole Taylorcraft because his partner hand-propped it, by himself, with the throttle mistakenly wide open and the wheels unchocked. Back on the ground astraddle the wheel again, holler Clear! and turn the crank. The impulse coupling snaps loudly, but no combustion ensues. One more turn on the crank and the five cylinders, one after another in the proper order, fire with confidence and not a little blue smoke, smattering my pants with spots of oil which had accumulated in the exhaust stack.

I reach up into the front cockpit and switch to both magnetos and then I carefully remove the crank, being sure to avoid the whirling propeller. They make nasty cuts, if not fatal ones. I always figured OSHA resents their not being able to put some kind of safety guard on the whirling propellers of airplanes. Of course the airplane would not then fly with said guard in place, but imagine trying to sell a table saw or a radial-arm saw without their myriad of requisite protective guards; no one would buy them. And yet, for more than a hundred years we have operated flying machines this way. I don't know if there is a point to be made by this observation, but perhaps it simply says that common sense is not completely dead after all.

Since I first purchased the Fleet, the range of emotions I experience is always the same when I start the engine. It begins with the anxiety of knowing I may not be using the right number of primer squirts given the ambient temperature, or I may not have the throttle open enough. And because of the long ago incident with that Taylorcraft, I sometimes check the throttle position four or five times. But when the engine fires and I reach into the front cockpit to switch from the left mag to both mags, enveloped in exhaust smoke, I am always smiling to myself. And if there are onlookers, as this seldom seen ritual is a curiosity at most airports, I am filled with pride that, yes, I am one of those patient, stubborn pilots who knows how to prop an antique biplane and who even enjoys it. And I may even know a thing or two about how that five-cylinder radial actually works. Because maybe I am also the mechanic who keeps it airworthy. Yes, that is something to be immensely proud of, especially since I did not grow up disassembling and reassembling my toys.

# CHAPTER FIVE

THE ENGINE WAS WARM now and we closed up my hangar; it looked huge inside without the Fleet parked in the middle of the battleship gray concrete floor. I imagined the Fleet was anxious to go, but surely it will miss the warm, dry Quonset hut home I erected for it three years prior. It is safe from all but tornadoes when parked inside. But for several days to come it will depend in part on my good judgment to keep it as safe as possible from the elements while flying to Kansas and back. Otherwise it will depend on good fortune and the whims of cold fronts and low pressure areas. But airplanes are not as vulnerable to the elements as some believe. After all, airplanes love for the wind to blow right in their faces. Indeed, they cannot leave the ground without enough wind across their wings.

I strapped my small clothes bag in the front seat with the safety belt and shoulder harness, then stepped over into the rear cockpit and strapped myself in. I waved goodbye to my friend standing by the soon-to-be lonely hangar and taxied to the west end of the grass runway to do a run-up. My strip is oriented almost perpendicular to a two-lane blacktop out in the country and the Fleet is the only airplane in the entire county, so it still draws attention when I take off to the east. A pick-up truck pulled over onto the shoulder. I felt some of that same pride as when I hand-prop the Kinner and I wondered if the people in the truck were wondering what I was doing or where I was going. Maybe one day they will stop to ask for an airplane ride, which I will gladly give them.

With firm pressure on the mechanical brakes, I eased the throttle forward to fourteen hundred revolutions and as the needle passed one thousand my oil pressure was still only a hundred pounds per square inch, so I knew the engine was sufficiently warm and would not exceed its RPM limitation at full power. I turned the switch to check each magneto individually and only saw a twenty RPM drop on each of them. Perfect. Another slight reduction in RPM told me the carb heat was working properly. A quick glance to be sure the oil cap was in place and off we went.

We were in the air in less than eight hundred feet, climbing into the headwind, and once we were safely above the tall pines I banked around to take up a northwesterly heading on the bobbing wet compass. As I passed back over the hangar I waved to my friend who was still watching. A thousand feet above the green, hazy farmland of Bertie County I leveled off and could see the big power line that leads right to Tri-County Airport where I would top off my gas tank. With a twenty knot tailwind, I was there in fifteen minutes and turned my base leg in the traffic pattern over the sad old U.S. Air Force trainer jet which was welded onto a pole and covered in bird crap. Thirty years ago local Boy Scouts would have clamored to keep it clean to earn some sort of community service merit badge, but these days no one seems to care how badly it looks. We touched down on the grass just outside the runway lights bordering the asphalt and taxied to the ramp.

I pulled the mixture and the Kinner coughed to a stop as my old flight instructor came out of the office, walking towards the Fleet. Henry had taught me to fly right here at this airport thirty-four years earlier when I was just out of high school, so I always stop to visit and buy gas on my way to wherever. I have never flown with him since then and I often wonder what he would think of my flying skills now. Would he notice the good habits he instilled in me so long ago? I have never once been in any cockpit, whether piston, turboprop, one engine or four, where I did not think of him and what he had shown me in that little Grumman. He is still passing on all that knowledge to students, thank goodness.

A full tank and I was off again to pick up my friend, Wayland, an hour and a half more to the west. It was smoother at a thousand feet than the wind on the ground indicated. But it was hazy and although I had flown that route before, I looked for the checkpoints on my chart to see if the wind was drifting the Fleet. We crossed the dark water of the winding Roanoke River a mile north of the prison, right on course. Looking down on the drab grey architecture of the prison, I imagined how demoralizing it would be to look out the window of your cell and see an open-cockpit biplane pass overhead, free in the sky. The wind was on our tail still and I secretly hoped it would stay that way all week, but I didn't count on it. Soon the new county airport outside Halifax went by off the right wing.

I could look slightly to the north and see the older airport it had replaced. That one is closer to town and is where my dad learned to fly on the GI Bill when he returned home from the Korean War. I barely remember going there with him when I was little. My mom likes to tell the story of how, when they returned from their honeymoon in Florida, my dad unceremoniously deposited her and her suitcase at her parents' doorstep and hauled ass to the airport to find out what he'd missed while he'd been gone. He loved airplanes and airports. He said that when he was a small child, his father would load the family in their car and drive to an airport just to watch the airplanes take off and land. I could be wrong, and I hope I am, but I don't think that is a common outing for families these days.

Hazy or not, the visibility was uncommonly good for the end of May and soon I saw the tall tower that overlooks Sky King Ranch, and just beyond, Ball Field. I planned on stopping to visit on the way home from Kansas but, for the time being, the Fleet and I continued on, still enjoying a twenty mile-per-hour tailwind.

Interstate 85 was right where it should be as we crossed over it north of Durham and way off to our left was the big Raleigh airport, the floor of its Class C airspace just a few hundred feet above us. I wondered if there was a passenger with a window seat in one of the commuter jets above us that was descending into the Raleigh-Durham Airport who looked down and unexpectedly saw the little yellow biplane. Did they wish they were in my front cockpit, or were they glad they were in the relative comfort of the jet? In another few minutes we were over more plowed farmland and an eastbound dust cloud behind a tractor belied the tailwind pushing us westward.

Even at a thousand feet above the ground, antennas and cell towers are a hazard and I was constantly lowering my goggles over my eyes so I could stick my head beyond my small windscreen to take a good look ahead of the airplane. I could not depend solely on what my chart said was not there. I always imagine a giant tower, erected months ahead of schedule, which somehow does not get included on the NOAA's latest chart data for that area. For pilots, I suppose it is a fine line between paranoia and thoroughness.

The small towns of Mebane and Hillsborough passed under the left wing and before long the bigger town of Burlington came into view. Just south of the interstate highway which passes through the town is the municipal airport, but we were close to our destination and didn't need any fuel yet. The small lakes northeast of Greensboro slowly came into view, so I started looking for the Air Harbor Airport. I've always thought that is a wonderfully fitting name for a small airport. When I saw Church Street winding north away from downtown, I traced it backwards until I found the side road which leads to the airpark. The small runway is hidden by all the trees in what is a rural residential area. At low altitudes, it's always hard to spot until you are almost over it. But soon there it was and we did a couple of circuits around the airport to check the field's condition. There was no other traffic and the field was in good condition, so we turned left base and set up for touching down on the grass at the west end.

I parked the Fleet on a level spot of grass that sloped down from a ramshackle barn hangar housing a lovely yellow Taylorcraft. I made a quick cellphone call to let Wayland and Jane know I had arrived and then I began tying down the Fleet. It was already in the mid-nineties and, as always, I wished I was still a thousand feet up in the air where it was cooler. By the time the Fleet was secure for the night, my friends had arrived and as we walked back toward the gravel parking lot I stopped to take a picture of the airplane in the barn. That barn had been put to good use and upon closer inspection I could see it wasn't as ramshackle as I'd thought. It had been shored up nicely and the little yellow Taylorcraft seemed happy inside it. That is a pleasing sight.

We spent the afternoon lying beside the inviting pool behind Wayland and Jane's house. Their backyard has that private, secret garden feeling to it, with the pool nestled in amongst the ample shade trees and hedges. I had flown the Fleet cross-country in the scorching hot summertime enough to appreciate a respite such as a cold beer and a refreshing swim. Anyone with less of a constitution for challenging road trips than Wayland would have given me pause for concern as my co-pilot. Accompanying an antique airplane halfway across the United States and back is a lot of work, albeit with great rewards.

So, we planned and philosophized on our upcoming adventure until we were waterlogged and the steaks were perfectly grilled. It was a delicious, satisfying meal with which to celebrate our much anticipated flight to western Kansas via the vast expanse of the Great Plains. But first we had to cross the Appalachian Mountains of western North Carolina, which we would do first thing in the morning.

# CHAPTER SIX

WE WOKE UP EARLY Sunday morning and ate a few sausage biscuits with our coffee before driving back over to Air Harbor. Our preflight uncovered no new concerns for us as we folded and stored the cockpit and engine covers along with our scant baggage. The Fleet was never meant to be a camping airplane so, with a passenger in each cockpit, there isn't much room available for gear. We each had a small handbag with as much clothing as would fit and still be storable around our feet and legs without interfering with the flight controls. My meager baggage compartment behind the rear cockpit was already packed full of tools and fluids, so whatever we could put in and around our seats was what we took with us.

I had learned on previous outings with the Fleet to simply pack enough clothes to get to my destination and then plan on buying new pants and shirts to wear on the return trip. Anything I wore would be covered in oil and grease after four or five days of flying anyway, so they would be cut up and used for work rags on the way home. It's quite an efficient system when you think about it.

There was a heavy dew on the Fleet but the sun was getting high and hot and it would soon be another day with no clouds. Satisfied that all our gear was secure, I gave Wayland a thorough tutorial on managing the engine controls in the front cockpit while I hand-propped the Kinner. He was a quick study and we soon rolled down the narrow asphalt runway at Air Harbor and then lifted into the humid, smooth air on our way to our first fuel stop in Elkin.

I was hoping the morning's flight would be a good omen weather wise. There was not a bump in the air and the midday haze had not yet formed; we could see downtown Winston-Salem as soon as we were airborne and I could just make out the opening in the trees that was the Smith-Reynolds Airport. We were still underneath Greensboro's Class C airspace as Brews Lake passed by on our right. When we crossed over the four-lane highway that ran up to Mt. Airy, Pilot Mountain was in plain view ahead of us. At more than two thousand feet above sea level, it was towering above us. Then we were following the course of the Yadkin River towards the Elkin Airport, which sat just east of Interstate 77 and northeast of town.

There was nobody talking on the Unicom frequency and there was no traffic in the pattern so we landed to the southwest and taxied to the avgas pump at the edge of the ramp. The flight had been less than an hour so we didn't really need a rest but, being early still, we had to wait more than an hour before someone showed up who could sell us some fuel. Eventually, we were airborne again and I wasted no time in offsetting the beautiful weather we were enjoying by getting us lost.

I intended to fly straight toward the town of Boone and cross the Blue Ridge Mountains into Tennessee through that pass and then follow the road over to Watauga Lake. Easy as pie, right? Wrong. The last time I remembered knowing exactly where I was was when we passed north of the Wilkes County airport. I can't honestly say why I didn't see the big four-lane highway beneath us that would have led the Fleet directly to Deep Gap and Boone. Or why I didn't recognize any landmarks on my sectional that would have helped point the way. But I didn't, so southwest we continued until finally it was time to do the right thing and land to ask for directions. Sure, I could blame Wayland for not being a better navigator, but he wasn't a licensed pilot, nor did he have charts in the front cockpit, so that wouldn't work. I could blame my hardheadedness for always wanting to navigate GPS-free with only a chart and an alcohol compass. No, I was just lost, which actually isn't so bad when the weather is nice and you have lots of gas in your fuel tank.

We were forty miles south of our intended course when I finally spotted a gorgeous, well-kept grass strip more than three thousand feet long. We landed to the west and noticed a fair-sized hangar with open doors as we taxied to a stop on a big grassy area near some T-hangars. I left the engine idling while Wayland held the brakes and I unbuckled and clamored over the side, chart in hand, and walked towards the occupied hangar. Two guys were walking towards me, asking if I needed any help.

"You could tell me where the hell I'm at!" I replied, trying to sound funny and humble at the same time.

Laughing, they told me it was Shiflet Field, near Marion, North Carolina. I told them I was trying to get up into Tennessee across the mountains north of us and was there a good pass without climbing too high? So they showed me the route we should take into Tennessee on my chart and I said goodbye and thanked them.

I noticed as I was talking with them that their hangar appeared to be a restoration facility for Republic Seabees, a classic amphibian airplane, and what got my attention was how organized and professional it appeared inside. There's just nothing as satisfying as seeing a clean, squared-away workshop. I wished we could've visited a while but I felt compelled to get across the Blue Ridge Mountains while the weather was so pleasant.

The route they showed me on the chart basically followed a railroad track that headed north out of Marion for a few miles and then wound its way up into the mountains. A fast flowing river ran exactly beside the tracks as we flew above them up into the narrow valley. It was definitely the scenic route across the mountains and the lovely weather only improved the view. The peaks on both sides of us were between four and five thousand feet high and we stayed well below the ridgelines as we traversed our way further into the hills.

The little towns sitting by the river seemed quaint and neat from our perch a thousand feet up. But, of course, they must with names like Spruce Pine and Little Switzerland. As always, I was looking down at the townspeople wondering how many were looking up at us wondering where the heck we were going in this contraption. Were we lost? Were we scared? Were we nuts?

Soon the railroad and its constant companion the river turned northwest and after another ten or twelve miles of breathtaking scenery I could make out the flatter terrain over in Tennesse. We would soon be across the Blue Ridge Mountains and out of North Carolina. A last turn around a high ridge to our right and the pass deposited us out onto the almost flatlands near the town of Erwin. We turned west toward our next fuel stop.

# CHAPTER SEVEN

EASTERN TENNESSEE WAS HOT and humid and the visibility was already diminished by the summertime haze when we touched down at the Greene County Airport near Greenville. After completing our fuel and oil ritual with the Fleet, we stood by the air-conditioning vent inside the FBO lobby while the young kid behind the counter processed my credit card. How did folks get by before there was air-conditioning? Would I rather do without soft, two-ply toilet paper or air-conditioning? I secretly hoped I would never be faced with that choice.

While enjoying the cool air coming out of the vent, we were approached by a middle-aged gentleman who was obviously a flight instructor and he had his young student in tow. They were on their way out to the ramp for a lesson and, after the what-the-heck-is-that inquiries regarding the Fleet, the instructor proceeded to expound, unsolicited by me, on the open-cockpit biplane experiences of a friend of his. Pilots, as a group, just are not modest people; they simply cannot forego an opportunity to indulge a willing audience with their past exploits or those of their friend or a distant acquaintance. In most cases, it is welcome, often even inspiring, information, but, in other cases such as this one, it just isn't.

To be honest, this instructor was trying way too hard to impress his young, impressionable student. I suppose that was his prerogative as the teacher but I've always found it to be an annoying behavior in pilots. On the other hand, I have to give credit where it's due; at least he was helping to teach a young person how to fly. You could not pay me enough money to climb into a small, cramped Cessna on a ninety-five degree afternoon to give flight instruction. I guess I'm too selfish with my time. And I'm lazy.

We soon departed the Greene County Airport and pointed the Fleet slightly northwest toward Kentucky. Twenty miles into our flight we started crossing some sharp razorback ridges on a diagonal and, looking back over my right shoulder, I could just make out through the hazy sky the runway of the New Tazewell Airport. I had stopped there in the Fleet the year before when I had been waylaid by thunderstorms while en route to Texas. There were some nice folks in New Tazewell who I'd hoped to visit on this trip, but we decided not to make time for a detour.

In this part of the state two big rivers, the Clinch and the Powell, flow down out of the northeast pretty much parallel to one another and empty into an expansive water recreation area called Norris Lake. It was full of boaters on this clear, sunny Sunday afternoon. Now, when I say boaters, I mean houseboaters. And when I say houseboaters, I mean that literally.

These folks have taken the concept of having a place on the lake and they have run with it. They build whole houses, porches and all, some even two stories tall, on floating platforms and just anchor them out on the lake. Row after row of them. It looks from a thousand feet in the air the way a neat, small-town neighborhood would look if it was flooded by rising water. I've never seen anything quite like it and I naturally wondered what they do with all their sewage.

After we had passed all the lakes and recreation areas, we found ourselves over flatter terrain; this was north-central Tennessee, almost into Kentucky. There was more pastureland beneath us now and only a few small towns scattered about. Then I noticed the town of Jamestown on my chart and it rang a bell; why was it so familiar?

While Wayland was in the middle of his first flight lesson, not a great idea on my part since the air was kind of bumpy, I studied the chart in the area around Jamestown a little more closely. Soon I noticed the small community of Pall Mall north of Jamestown and then I remembered. Pall Mall was the birthplace of Sergeant Alvin York, winner of the Medal of Honor in World War One, and a genuine son of the Volunteer State, still highly revered nearly a hundred years later and well he should be.

One of my favorite classic films of all time is *Sergeant York*, where Gary Cooper is the humble, unassuming York. I had always heard that back in 1945 the movie premiered in the nearby bigger town of Jamestown because it was the nearest place to Pall Mall that had a movie house. Sounds plausible, in fact, I think that's still the case today. So, you just never know what you're going to fly over, even when you're seemingly over the middle of nowhere. On the other hand, when you travel by air you can't stop just anywhere and go exploring, unless of course there happens to be an airport handy.

We had a fair headwind and weren't going to make it quite as far as we'd planned on this leg, so I started looking for an alternate fuel stop on my chart. That is, in between pushing the nose back over and leveling the wings throughout Wayland's ongoing first flying lesson. In all fairness, he was doing reasonably well since he had never flown an airplane before, but we experienced pilots sometimes take holding a heading and an altitude for granted. Even though the Fleet was designed as a primary trainer for the military back in 1941, by today's standards it just isn't ideal for instructing. The wind noise in the open cockpits isn't conducive to giving a lecture regarding the finer points of piloting.

Now, I'm a fairly patient person, up to a point, compassionate even, but I was getting airsick. But I persevered a bit longer; after all, the first time an aspiring student pilot flies an antique biplane across northern Tennessee on a lovely, summer afternoon should be a special, cherished moment. I thought of the flight instructor back in Greenville and admitted to myself what a saint he was, pretentious storytelling or not.

We were only averaging sixty miles-per-hour across the ground thanks to the headwind, but after almost two hours of flying we crossed into Kentucky. Each time we crossed one of the big dotted lines on the sectional chart that represented a state boundary, I thought about Tom Sawyer and his first hot air balloon ride. He thought each state would be a different color like on the maps in his school books. Or was that Huck Finn? When we were kids, my sister and I had a jigsaw puzzle of the United States. All the pieces were made of plastic and each state had a color; as I recall, Tennessee was yellow. Today it had been hazy green, if that's a color.

Just past the Cumberland River we spotted the Monroe County Airport near Tompkinsville. It sat out in the rural countryside surrounded by grassy, rolling hills and we were hoping there was gas and oil for sale.

# CHAPTER EIGHT

ALTHOUGH THE RAMP WAS hotter than blue blazes, we at least found a self-service pump for avgas, but no oil. The FBO seemed fairly new and well-kept but it was unattended, so we weren't going to be purchasing any oil. I was starting to suspect a flaw in our overall trip planning. It was Memorial Day weekend and I had assumed most FBOs would be open throughout the three-day weekend, but we would find that my assumption was greatly in error.

Fortunately I always keep five or six quarts of oil in my baggage compartment for just such an emergency. Like Foghorn's feathers. The Kinner was burning a little over a quart an hour, which is not excessive and, in fact, has remained consistent throughout the engine's life, which has spanned more than three hundred hours of operation.

After Wayland and I did our hand-prop dance, we got situated in our respective cockpits and taxied to the runway just as a little Robinson helicopter was departing to the southeast, the occupants waving to us. But we pointed our nose west toward southern Illinois in hopes of reaching Paducah or thereabouts before dark. This was the hottest part of the day and I generally prefer to layover for a while in an air-conditioned FBO lobby and get to know the airport manager but, with nobody around, we had no choice but to push on.

Half an hour of flying in smooth air put us south of Bowling Green as we crossed over Interstate 65 with all its Memorial Day traffic trudging north and south. We were only a thousand feet high so, as always, I wondered who in the cars and trucks below might be looking up at us. And, if so, were they at all fascinated to see an old yellow biplane? Did any children in the back seat of their parents' car point us out? Or were they too immersed in their ipods or the movie playing on the screen built into the back of the headrests in front of them? I'll never know of course, but I like to think some child saw us and promised themselves they too would go barnstorming one day. Or perhaps they would be compelled to ask their parents to buy them an airplane ride in the near future.

Another thirty minutes had us skimming across the northern edge of Fort Campbell's big Alert Area just north of Hopkinsville and there was another interstate below us which was pretty much paralleling our westward course. The weather was still cooperating as there were only a few small cumulus clouds scattered in the distance and there were no dark buildups in any direction. The Fleet is a fair weather flying machine only and I never try to outrun or out climb anything. Not that I could if I wanted to at seventy-five miles-per-hour. My flight planning philosophy with the Fleet is to take off in VFR weather with three hours of fuel on board with the intention of being somewhere in two hours with more than one airport to choose from at which to land. At such a slow cruise speed I'm never going to overtake any weather that I can't see coming for miles around. And, while not impossible, as I'd already proven, it's kind of hard to get lost going so slowly. It's sort of the opposite of what the fighter pilots say about how you've never been lost until you've been lost at Mach 2.

Someone once asked me why I never carry a portable GPS for navigation and instead rely only on a chart and my wet compass. My answer is that I simply enjoy finding my way with a sectional chart, the wet compass, a plotter, and my watch. To me, dead reckoning and pilotage are to piloting what dope and fabric work is to airplane maintenance. It's nostalgia, a lost art. If I start out with a full tank of gas, which I always do, and good weather as far as I can see, I always have plenty of time to find myself even when I'm temporarily confused as to my whereabouts. Add to that a heaping helping of common sense and good judgment and it's pretty hard to screw up.

Besides, I get to use all the latest cockpit gadgets and gizmos at my real job so it's refreshing, not to mention challenging, to fly across America with a needle and ball and alcohol compass as my primary flight instruments. On any given day in the United States I wonder how many pilots are taking a trip somewhere in this fashion? Probably not too many. For me, and I know this will seem corny, to navigate in this fashion is also a tribute to all the pilots, men and women alike, who pioneered the skies between the east and west coasts between the two world wars. Not to mention between Europe and North America over the forbidding Atlantic Ocean. Come to think of it, maybe it's the spirit of those accomplishments that inspires pilots and mechanics to keep antique aircraft flying, even if it's just to fly them around the patch on a calm summer evening. At least I hope that's part of the reason.

Two hours of watching the green hills and forests of western Kentucky pass underneath put us over two huge water recreation areas. One was Lake Barkley and the other was Kentucky

Lake and they were full of boaters enjoying the holiday weekend. Each body of water constituted its own state park and it looked to me like some tributaries of the Ohio River had been dammed up to form them. To be honest, I was secretly wishing I was down there in a big inner tube drinking a cold beer. Right on cue, Wayland piped up on the intercom and said he suspected there were hot dogs grilling as well as coolers of ice cold beer right below us. After a long, hot day of fueling and oiling we were envious of those people on the lakes. You never have a float plane when you need one.

The Kentucky Dam State Park Airport was the logical place at which to stop but even from the downwind leg of the traffic pattern I could see that it might very well be unattended. I was starting to suspect that these airport managers had themselves a union. Sure enough, this airport too was abandoned and devoid of any services whatsoever. There was not even a water fountain. Most importantly, there wasn't a self-service gas pump, so I didn't even shut down the engine and we taxied back to the runway and took off.

On we went and within a few miles we crossed the Ohio River, which forms Kentucky's entire northern and western border with four states, meandering from West Virginia to Illinois. The town of Paducah was coming into view on the south side of the big river. Our destination now though was the little airport in Metropolis, Illinois, on the north bank of the river.

Due to our oversight regarding the scarcity of functioning FBOs on this most noble of holidays, I was invoking the inherent logic of my flight planning philosophy. That is, always land with an hour's worth of fuel remaining. But now I had used up one fourth of that reserve getting to the Metropolis airfield, which was my personal limit for comfort in the Fleet. Mr. Murphy however was not on holiday. The giant mural of Superman painted on the side of what I could only assume was the main building on the field at Metropolis was a misnomer, as I would not use *super* as a prefix in describing anything I saw. This airfield had seen better days and on this day was in fact deserted. I shut the Kinner off; we were going to have to scrounge up some gas and oil.

Speaking of Mr. Murphy, it never ceases to amaze me how when on those days where you're just not in the mood to expound on what type aircraft you're flying, where you're headed, or where you've come from, everybody in town seems to show up at the airport to investigate the little yellow biplane and ask a million questions. But land somewhere in dire need of some assistance and there is not a soul to be found. Or the few people who drive by don't even seem to notice the Fleet, which is not exactly a common airplane at most airfields. Well, this was one of those days.

There were a few short rows of hangars not far from where we had parked so we put the gust lock on the rudder, chocked the tires, and walked over to investigate. One hangar had a sign advertising the sale of Aeroshell oil, which was just the oil we needed. It was locked and there were no phone numbers posted on the door. Wayland walked back to the airplane to keep an eye on the airport driveway in case someone drove up who could help. I walked to the south end of the runway where some houses were situated in a nearby neighborhood. I was hot and tired after a long day of flying but we needed gas if we were getting the hell out of Metropolis, home of Superman or not. Even a ride to a nearby filling station would suffice since the Kinner engine can legally burn automobile fuel as long as it contains no ethanol. There was nobody home at those houses.

Back at the Fleet, trying to enjoy the shade cast by the top wing, we pondered our options. Neither of us had a smartphone with access to the internet with which we could conjure up a taxi and a motel room. Nor were there any numbers posted on any of the doors or windows around the concrete airport office. Obviously, my habit of trying not to conduct our adventure in too regimented a fashion by avoiding strict timetables, planned fuel stops, and room reservations, was biting us in the butt.

About then a dark blue pickup truck pulled into the airport driveway and parked at one of the hangars we had previously investigated. We hurried on down there to introduce ourselves. The very agreeable gentleman sold us several quarts of oil and ten gallons of avgas he already had stored inside his hangar in cans. We paid him cash on the barrelhead and this fine fellow pilot, saint that he was, carried us and our loot in his truck back to where our airplane was parked.

There is something about being flush with gas and oil in such circumstances that completely alters your mood from slightly disgusted to downright buoyant. We could now get airborne again and begin our search for some decent accommodations for ourselves and the Fleet for the evening. We decided to fly back south across the Ohio River into Kentucky and land at the Barkley Regional Airport west of Paducah. I generally avoid having to talk to air traffic controllers in my biplane because, while I can hear them just fine in my headset, they often have a difficult time understanding my transmissions due to wind noise in the open cockpit. So, as a courtesy, I normally don't land at airports with control towers.

But apparently Murphy had become bored with us and had gone on his merry way because we had an unexpectedly pleasant flight over to Barkley Regional. The hot sun, which had added to our fatigue throughout the day ever since we had left Greenville, Tennessee, was now only half an hour from setting and the evening was smooth and silky, perfect for flying. Sadly, this leg barely lasted twenty minutes but you have to savor these magic moments as they present themselves when flying. I relaxed and enjoyed the scenery on a long five-mile final to Runway 22, exchanging radio calls with a very friendly controller who, thankfully, had no problem understanding me.

While they are never aesthetically pleasing when your mission is to seek out strange, new grass airstrips, the truth is that the presence of a modern fixed-base operator usually means you can find what you need in the way of services. And that's just what we found at the MidContinent FBO, in spite of the fact that we taxied into our parking spot just as they were closing for the evening. The young kid who operated the fuel truck even gave us a ride into town once we had fully serviced the Fleet and covered it snugly for the night. It looked out of place on the ramp, surrounded by the sleek, metal, piston-powered airplanes and business jets. It had safely brought us a long way from home since early that morning and it deserved a rest. And we deserved a hot shower and a cold beer.

# CHAPTER NINE

NEVER UNDERESTIMATE THE RE-CUPERATIVE powers of a good night's sleep, preceded by a T-bone steak and a pitcher of Miller Lite. The next morning promised to be another clear flying day and, with a substantial continental breakfast under our belts, we checked out of the hotel and called a local taxi for a ride back out to the airport.

While I checked the regional weather on the handy computers in the lobby of the FBO, Wayland walked out to the Fleet and started removing the covers. It was sitting right where we had left it like a good bird dog. Our long, seven-hour cross-country of the previous day meant I had to grease the rocker arms on each of the five cylinders this morning. So, while Wayland folded and stowed the covers, I prepared my grease gun which is always a messy undertaking. Part of the messiness was the fact that I had to remove practically every item in the small baggage compartment to get to the grease gun. You wouldn't think you could pack so much stuff into such a small space.

I enjoy greasing the rocker arms on the Kinner. It falls into the same category as pilotage and fabric repairs. It makes me feel close to my engine, which after all is the key to the whole deal, and it gives me an opportunity to scrutinize all the nooks and crannies before asking of it another long day of flying. This simple ceremony reminds me, lest I forget, that I'm being transported across America in a unique flying machine that deserves being pampered and not taken for granted.

By the time I was done, Wayland had the engine cover folded flat and stowed behind my seat cushion and the cockpit cover was rolled up and bungeed to the cross tubes on the floor near my control stick. In an airplane designed only as a trainer, it takes some ingenuity to safely stow all our gear. Eventually we were ready to start the motor, which is my favorite part of the entire process.

There was a middle-aged couple who had been preflighting their spotless Cessna 182 the entire time we'd been out on the ramp. They were just a few parking spaces down from us and had been surreptitiously watching our lengthy preparations, yet they had never walked over to strike up a conversation. There is no way I could watch someone prepare an old biplane for what was obviously a serious undertaking and not stroll over to say hello. Now, I don't presume to assign any importance whatsoever to ourselves or to our little adventure, but come on. It's just not something you see every day, especially at a controlled airfield with not another fabric-covered airplane in sight, least of all an open-cockpit biplane. Maybe they were just a bit shy. Maybe we were giving off unsociable vibes, though not hardly. Or maybe they just didn't give a crap. I guess it's possible.

My front-seater held the brakes and stood by the magneto switch as I cranked the thick wooden propeller. The sweet, blue, smoke-tinged rhythm of all five cylinders filled my head as I climbed, smiling, into the rear seat. It was another soft, calm flying morning with no clouds in sight and very little haze. The controller in the tower sounded like the guy from the evening before, but I wasn't sure. He cleared us to the end of the runway nearest our parking area and we taxied to the yellow hold line for a run-up. All systems were go, what few there are on the Fleet, and we trundled down the centerline, got airborne, and banked to the west just in time to pass by the top of the control tower, waving good morning and goodbye to the gentleman inside.

Smooth as silk is how I would unoriginally describe the morning's first leg of flying; the kind of flight you don't want to end. I could see by the contented look on my friend's face beneath his goggles that he was in full agreement. Neither of us spoke for a while, as if we didn't want to disrupt the other's enjoyment of the morning's flight.

Twenty-five miles further west we passed just north of Cairo, Illinois, which is at the southernmost tip of the state, situated on a small peninsula jutting into the confluence of the Ohio and Mississippi Rivers. I wondered if the town's name was somehow inspired by past events on these storied waterways. We actually crossed over the wide Mississippi three times in the course of ten miles, as it almost doubled back on itself twice before turning north to form the state of Missouri's eastern border. That old river had a lot of stories it could tell. Looking down on it, I wondered how many people had floated downstream on its powerful current in the past several centuries. And for some reason it made me think of Mark Twain and what humor he would have found in looking up and seeing a flying machine pass over his head.

Once beyond the big rivers, we were well into our long flight across southern Missouri; it would take us at least three legs of flying to reach Kansas, which was our goal for the day. The elevation of the hills below was about five hundred feet above sea level and the morning air remained smooth. There were only a few scattered communities beneath us; it was definitely not a heavily populated part of the state. Eventually we crossed perpendicularly to a newly-constructed four-lane highway and I was able to pinpoint our location on my chart. The absence of crosswinds had made navigating easy so far, but we were going to have to stop for gas before the two-hour mark because, according to my sectional chart, airports would be scarce farther along our preferred route.

So I began searching for a rock quarry denoted on my chart which would help point the way to the small town of Piedmont, Indiana, nestled in a narrow hill valley not far from a big horseshoe-shaped lake. It wasn't long before I spotted the quarry, which is always a reliable checkpoint for VFR pilots, and we turned south to follow the nearby winding railroad tracks into Piedmont.

The small town was laid out lengthwise in the narrow valley between two ridges with the Black River running through the valley bottom.

The tiny municipal airport was at the south end of town so we had to fly right above the main street as we approached the traffic pattern from the north. My hope was that someone who was part of the local aviation community would see us passing overhead and drive out to the airport to investigate. I didn't want to be stranded again like in Metropolis, after all, today was Memorial Day.

Sure enough, much to our relief, a man was pulling up to the modest airport office building in his pick-up truck just as we taxied to a stop at the self-service avgas pump. He introduced himself as Jeff and said he'd seen us fly over town and so he had come out to see who and what was dropping in. Now that's more like it.

Jeff said he ran an auto parts store in town and was one of several volunteer airport managers. A very friendly fellow and quite fascinated by our trip, he was genuinely thrilled to have us stop and visit their airport. He was also a wealth of information regarding local grass strips and other antique taildragger owners in the area. A friend of Jeff's and his co-pilot wife taxied by after landing in their Cessna 172. They were returning from a cross-country trip and walked down to the fuel pumps to say hello after they had put their Cessna in its T-hangar behind the airport office.

Wayland and I finished fueling and oiling as we talked with our newfound pilot friends who provided us with what we hoped would be good advice as to where we might or might not find avgas on our upcoming leg to Springfield. They made a couple of phone calls to FBOs they were familiar with to see who was open or closed since the holiday weekend was still in full swing. In the end, we all decided the Springfield Downtown Airport would be our best bet; it was two hours away. We were reminded by the Cessna pilot and his wife to keep an eye out for the tall towers east of the city. Excellent advice.

We cranked up, strapped in, and taxied to the north end of the paved runway, waving to our new friends as we S-turned along the taxiway. There wasn't any wind to help us on our climbout and it was already ninety degrees at ten-thirty in the morning. The Fleet always gets into the air easily but it doesn't necessarily climb very well. My reason for departing to the south therefore was because of several big pastures along the river in that direction; I had seen them when we were landing. For emergencies during take-off to the north however, there would only be Main Street.

I held the brakes and added power. We were off the ground in less than a thousand feet but, as I'd expected, our climb performance was not impressive. I kept the nose down to accelerate as much as possible before having to pull up to clear the trees in front of us beyond the end of the runway. We cleared them sufficiently, but not with the margin I generally prefer.

"All that propeller has to do is keep turning," I kept saying to myself.

That's what I always mumble on all such take-offs. Just keep turning happily and everything will be fine. And really that is the bottom line, isn't it? The propeller turns, the air flows sufficiently where it should and, voila, you are a contented, relaxed pilot slipping the surly bonds with a smile on your face rather than a grimace.

# CHAPTER TEN

OUR NEXT HOUR OF flying was over a kind of miniature badlands, bisected by the Current River, which flowed all the way down into Arkansas. It was a beautiful landscape full of craggy hills and cliffs that went right to the river's edge and the curving river was strewn with rocky rapids and inviting sandbars all along its course. But the air at a thousand feet above the ground had become turbulent and I was working harder than usual to keep the wings level. No doubt the quickly warming air rising from the rough terrain below us was the culprit. I was hoping it wouldn't be like that for the entire flight to Springfield.

Halfway there and finally beyond the rough air over the scenic river, we saw the four-lane highway that would lead us to our destination. It came up from the south but then turned west about where we crossed it; it was the perfect navigation aid. There were three small municipal airports, one after the other, ten or twelve miles apart along the big highway and after we had passed over the last one, I spotted the tall towers the pilot couple had warned us about back in Piedmont.

There were five of them and they were indeed tall; the tallest reached to thirty-five hundred feet above sea level. It's a little disconcerting looking up at a man-made structure from an open-cockpit biplane that towers more than a thousand feet above your head. To be honest, it actually gives me a queasy feeling in my stomach, even though I have no qualms about looking over the side of the Fleet from any height.

I steered northwest to give the towers a wider berth and then we followed an interstate highway for a few miles, which led us directly to the downtown airport. We assumed, wrongly again, that this airport would be doing business on Memorial Day weekend, especially since it was so close to a town the size of Springfield. Even more confusing though was the presence of a two thousand-foot tower immediately beside the approach end of Runway 29; I have never seen anything like that on an airport before. Clearly, they never intend to establish an instrument approach procedure into their airport.

But they did have a thirty mile-per-hour crosswind and my right tire protested a bit as I touched down on it first, with my right wing low. The runway wasn't overly wide either and I worked a little harder than usual to bring us to a stop and then turn around to back taxi. I think that might be the strongest direct crosswind I've ever landed in with the Fleet. So imagine my disgust with myself when, as we taxied toward the ramp, I noticed they had a nice wide turf runway bisecting the asphalt runway, and it was oriented directly into the wind!

There was not a soul to be found at the locked up FBO building; I'll plan better next time, as this was getting old after two days of barely finding gas and oil. Thankfully though there was a self-service fuel pump, so we only needed to find some oil. Fortunately for us, a curious amateur photographer wandered over to snap some photos of the Fleet and he happened to keep an airplane in one of the nearby hangars. He graciously sold us a few quarts of oil. We may have been experiencing a shortage of operating FBOs, but there was certainly no shortage of airport Samaritans.

We didn't socialize too long and were soon on our way; we still wanted to make Kansas at a decent hour. Hopefully we could stop and see an old friend near Wichita if our timing was good. I opted to use the paved runway again for take-off after a local pilot at the gas pump had told us there were some potholes on the grass strip. As much as I wanted to use the grass and depart directly into the strong wind, discretion is the better part of valor when you are such a long way from home.

So we crabbed along the centerline of Runway 29 and climbed skyward. I banked left as soon as the towers off our left wing allowed room for a safe turn and then we headed north while staying just below Springfield's Class C airspace. We turned west toward Kansas as soon as we were clear of the city and the nearby larger airport's traffic area.

Navigating was easier now that we were further west. The seemingly endless section lines were beginning to appear below us. For the most part they ran conveniently east and west, one mile apart, and they aid tremendously in holding cardinal headings with a wet compass. Since surveyors mapped much of America's Midwest using these lines, roads and highways were naturally built on top of them.

In spite of not being heavily populated, this leg of our trip had some other excellent landmarks in addition to the section lines. The huge Y-shaped Stockton Lake was not far off our right wing after leaving the Springfield area. Then for twenty or thirty miles there was only slightly rolling Missouri countryside before we crossed perpendicularly to a four-lane highway which paralleled a railroad track. Knowing that you're navigating toward something as prominent as a big river or a highway, which can't be confused with any other landmark, is quite comforting. It's never a matter of finding it but rather a matter of where you cross it relative to your plotted course.

Today we were right on course and passed over Highway 71 just south of the town of Lamar. Another fifteen minutes of enjoying our last views of western Missouri and the town of Pittsburg, Kansas, came into view. We had only flown an hour and a half but we knew there was no fuel at the next airport along our route, so we hoped Pittsburg could provide us with the services we needed.

The longer of the two paved runways allowed me to land into the strong wind which was no doubt kin to the one blowing back in Springfield. And, of course, as we taxied to a stop in front of the neatly kept FBO building, we could plainly see the sign on the door which read CLOSED. And why shouldn't it be? Everyone knows that only fools fly from town to town across America on Memorial Day weekend in need of oil and avgas so they can continue on their foolish way.

That's when I spied an open hangar behind the terminal building which appeared to have live humans moving about inside. Apparently they, like us, didn't honor the holiday by going to the lake. I had not shut off the motor yet so I added power and taxied to the front of the private hangar and again left Wayland onboard to hold the brakes. There was a man on an aircraft tug with a business jet in tow who waved back as I said hello.

I asked him if anyone was available to sell us some gas and oil. He said the airport manager, Bill, would gladly drive out on his day off if we gave him a call. The tug driver called Bill for us and then told us it would be about twenty minutes. Sweet! I thanked him and walked back to the Fleet, climbed in, and we taxied back to park in front of the terminal building and shut down.

It was now hot enough to fry eggs on the concrete in spite of the stiff breeze, but we began pouring what oil we had into the oil tank while waiting for Bill. They had no self-service gas pumps here and used fuel trucks instead. I was hoping they had not turned off the air-conditioning in the airport building over the weekend and that the drink machine was still plugged in. If they had a vending machine with snacks and a restroom with toilet paper, well, we would just be swimming in gravy.

Right on time, Bill showed up in exactly twenty minutes and indeed seemed happy to have been called out to the airport to help us. Many folks would have been irritated at being summoned from home for such a purpose, but not Bill. He was genuinely happy to come out and be of some service, for which we were very grateful. After fueling from the airport truck and adding more oil, we walked into the FBO. The cold air was like an angel's breath and the drink machine had ice cold root beer. I wanted to spend the night right there in the lobby.

I should mention that my friend, Wayland, while a very seasoned traveler, is not the most patient of travelers. I can linger at an airport such as Pittsburg for hours, even days. I'm of the mind that when you finally stumble onto a hospitable place, you should bask in it as long as possible. Wayland however likes to keep moving, although, to be honest, the fact that we were trying to meet our friend in Wichita before dark was probably contributing to his impatience.

So, I inhaled a last deep breath of air-conditioning and walked back out to the ramp after saying thanks and goodbye to Bill. Wayland was waiting beside the Fleet, feigning patience. By now he was an expert brake holder and grand high guardian of the magneto switch, so we were soon ready to taxi out to the active runway with the Kinner chugging along nicely. We both waved to Bill as we rolled away from the terminal building. Our destination was Beaumont, Kansas, a place that had been the impetus thirty years earlier to have my own open-cockpit biplane.

# CHAPTER ELEVEN

ACTUALLY, SEVEN YEARS EARLIER I had almost made it to Beaumont in my Fleet. My wife and I had purchased the Fleet one winter and the following summer we flew across the Deep South to northern Arizona and then back across the Rockies and the Midwest. That's an adventure for another book, but, to my great disappointment, Beaumont was the one place on our entire trip where we could not land due to widespread thunderstorms one evening. We had to detour south into Oklahoma before being able to turn east again.

In the seven years since, I have not tried again to fly to Beaumont until the day Wayland and I took off from Pittsburg, Kansas. But the skies were blue and clear and this time I was confident I would make it. As the crow flies, it was about a hundred miles to Beaumont and should take a little under two hours. A railroad track led us slightly northwest out of Pittsburg to a little place called Fredonia which was a little past the halfway point. The railroad continued to meander north of the course line I had drawn on my chart though, so we turned a little more westerly for another twenty-five miles. Then we crossed a small, kidney-shaped lake near the Neosho River and slightly south of a tiny township called St. Paul. That meant we were right on course with no crosswind at all and only a slight headwind. If things didn't change significantly we would be in Beaumont in another forty-five minutes of flying.

At a thousand feet above the ground we could see the rolling hills of eastern Kansas slowly becoming the undulating expanse of the Great Plains. The land below us was finally opening up; we were getting out West. The hills only rose two or three hundred feet above the surrounding prairie but they rolled on as far as we could see. Whether in the Fleet or in an airliner, I'm always in awe of the vastness of America. When I look down over the side of my cockpit, I imagine a caravan of covered wagons bound for Oregon a hundred and fifty years earlier, or a band of Native Americans on horseback chasing a buffalo herd. What a majestic country we live in. And, even more special for us pilots, we are free to roam above it and explore it in a privately owned and operated aircraft, relatively unhindered by oppressive regulations.

I descended to five hundred feet above the ground so we could better see the land below. Sand-colored outcroppings were scattered throughout the grasslands and there were occasional foundations of old home places, now in ruins. Naturally, I wondered who had lived there, way out here on the prairie? And what had happened to them? Where did they go and where are their descendants today?

In another twenty minutes the highway under our right wing would lead us straight to our destination. We could see a huge windmill farm in the distance that was actually five or six miles south of Beaumont and the tall wind turbines reached a hundred feet above our altitude. And before long, there it was. The grass strip owned by the Beaumont Hotel ran north and south on the eastern edge of the tiny town; the highway we had followed was perpendicular to its north end. I flew a circle around the town just to see where everything was located, particularly the road which led from the airfield to the hotel. The nation's oldest wooden water tower still in operation, previously used to service the Frisco Railroad in the town's heyday, stood proudly next to the historic hotel.

We touched down on the soft grass and taxied to the south end of the field. I hadn't flown all that way to not taxi down the public road and park by the hotel I had read about so many years before. The runway sloped slightly downward to where it ended at the narrow paved road, so we turned right and headed into town. About a quarter mile ahead I could see a stop sign protruding out of the grass along the shoulder of the road and it occurred to me that a low-wing airplane would have a problem here if its wing span was much greater than mine. But, to be fair, we were doing this at our own risk, at least according to a sign we passed that clearly stated no one except us would be responsible for anything since the beginning of time while we taxied down this road. Good ol' fault-free America; we sometimes have to take the bad with the good I suppose.

At the intersection I came to a complete stop, looked both ways, and continued straight ahead to a grassy area across the street from the historic Beaumont Hotel. A car had stopped at the stop sign too, but remained at the corner to watch us go by. We waved to its occupants and then I spun the Fleet's tail around and shut the engine off. We had made it, it was hot as hell, and the damn hotel was closed.

Son of a gun! I would've paid a hundred dollars for a frosty mug of draft beer at that very moment. No surprise to us by now, but the hotel was closed for Memorial Day just like all the FBOs along our route. It occurred to me then that businesses like that should offer self-service, credit card-only beer taps on occasions where they can't be there in person to serve the thirsty public. Much like all the self-service avgas pumps which had served us so well since we had left Air Harbor. It's probably an idea ahead of its time.

By now the couple who had been in the car at the stop sign had walked over to take some pictures of the Fleet. The man was a school teacher from Wichita and was totally enthralled by our journey. He and his wife had driven out to see the historic hotel and water tower. They too were surprised to find that the hotel was closed.

Wayland and I looked around the outside of the hotel and peered through the front glass, wishing we could go in and eat lunch. Instead, we sat in the shade on the front porch and rested a while, answering questions about our journey for the school teacher and his wife. We told them about our reasons for revisiting Greensburg, Kansas, after having been there five years before.

It was soon time to amble back out to the Fleet, look it over a bit, and add some oil. We were due at Stearman Field to meet our friend, Larry, for dinner. The Beaumont Hotel would be a wonderful stopover for airplane people on their way to anywhere. I will definitely have to land there again in order to enjoy the full experience of the hotel's hospitality and I can't afford to wait another thirty years to do it either. At least now I have seen the place and have taxied the Fleet into town like in the story I'd read when I was in college.

# CHAPTER TWELVE

STEARMAN FIELD, NEAR BENTON, Kansas, would be the greatest unscheduled find of our entire trip. It was an unexpected jewel of an airpark at which we were only stopping for a bite to eat and wound up spending the night and not wanting to leave, not even Wayland.

Before departing the grass strip at Beaumont, we had called our friend, Larry, to ascertain where he wanted to meet us for dinner. He suggested we meet him at the airfield restaurant on Stearman Field. "Oh, it's the neatest place!" he'd told us enthusiastically. "Lots of warbirds!"

I was a little skeptical at first. God bless those warbird guys and the beautiful airplanes they preserve, but they can be a cliquish bunch sometimes. And I've just never been able to get my mind around the whole olive drab flight suit-with-bogus-insignia thing. But what the heck? It was a place I'd never been with the Fleet and that was the whole purpose of this adventure, so we took off.

A northwest heading took us toward Benton and it was almost late afternoon so the temperature was decreasing a little, but not much. We soon started seeing our checkpoints that I'd marked on my chart as we crossed a railroad track running southwest out of El Dorado with an interstate highway roughly paralleling it a few miles away. Farther west we could make out the city of Wichita spread out across the flatness of the prairie. A lot of aviation history had taken place in the skies above that town since the early twentieth century. Clyde Cessna, Walter Beech, Lloyd Stearman, all the early greats. What an exciting, productive time that must have been for the engineers, pilots, and mechanics of all those fledgling companies, many of which are long gone now. To have been a young kid wanting to learn to fly, it must have been magical just to be near all of that early aviation industry. Of course, today wasn't a bad day to be there either.

We flew over Stearman Field to get the layout of the place and I could see the restaurant at the north end. The joint was already hopping with cars in the parking lot and seven or eight aircraft parked on the airplane ramp in front of the patio, which was full of patrons. What a welcome surprise to see an airport not only open for business, but downright festive.

There was a grass airstrip that paralleled the paved runway but I chose not to use it before talking to a local pilot; you just never know what might lurk there. While taxiing towards the restaurant we passed hangar after hangar with open doors and they were each filled with all manner of aircraft. There were people inside the hangars milling around or either sitting out front in chairs watching airplanes land. They all waved enthusiastically and we waved back.

I parked in a tie-down spot near the outdoor patio of the Stearman Cafe and we saw immediately the place was indeed packed. I guess everybody in these parts didn't go to the lake for Memorial Day. Some tall mugs of beer on many of the tables did not go unnoticed either. I was quickly warming to Stearman Field and so was Wayland. We were hot and tired and hungry and suddenly not so concerned with making it all the way to Greensburg by nightfall.

After chocking the Fleet and giving it a good looking over, we walked over to the front porch of the cafe and immediately saw our friend, Larry, standing at the railing. We had last seen him five years earlier when we had driven from North Carolina to cook pigs for the Greensburg, Kansas, Fourth of July gathering. The celebration had taken place one month after an F5 tornado had stomped that town flat. Larry had been born and raised in Greensburg and had been instrumental in making that bittersweet event possible. He was now a retired restaurateur, still enjoying life with a wide grin on his face. The first order of business was to get seated inside where there was air-conditioning and the second was to order some food.

Wayland and Larry each enjoyed a tall glass of beer as I sadly sipped iced tea. I was not sure if I would need to crank the Fleet and move it to a different parking spot before dark, so I had to abstain. Now, I know it may seem that I obsess over drinking beer at every turn and, in truth, I suppose I do. But for me, beer is one of life's simple pleasures which I neither take for granted nor abuse. There are certain strict guidelines regarding alcohol consumption, actually they are federal laws, which we must never violate as pilots in order to avoid severe consequences. But beer should not be taboo, even at airports.

I once hauled skydivers at a commercial parachute center in my younger years and those rowdy ne'er-do-wells loved to party. But the boss, Paul, had one simple rule: Nobody opens a beer until all the flying is done for the day and all the airplanes are tied down. Period. No exceptions. Ever. The rule was inviolable unless you wanted to be persona non grata on Paul's property for life. There were plenty of alcohol-related incidents, I mean, we're talking about skydivers, but none that had anything to do with aircraft or flying. I've always thought Paul's rule was a reasonable one and I try to adhere to its underlying philosophy of common sense whenever airplanes and alcohol are in close proximity.

The Stearman Cafe is one of the most tastefully appointed airport restaurants I've ever seen. The building itself is a former hangar which had also been an airplane dealership at one time. When the huge glass-framed doors are raised at each corner, a wonderful semi-outdoor seating area is created. Or, you can sit inside the bar's dining area, as we did. The views of the ramp and the northern approach end of the runway are nicely unobstructed. There is also a covered outdoor bandstand used for live music venues.

The decor is perfectly aeronautical, but not too corny, as are some airport cafes. There are lots of airplane memorabilia hanging from the ceiling which require some time to peruse. The most unique piece they have is an old Stearman wing hanging directly above the bar itself, home to a myriad of glass beer mugs.

All of this charming aviation atmosphere is the brainchild of Dwayne and Julie, who own the entire airpark. The airfield has been there for quite some time, but they purchased it recently and began making extensive improvements. I cannot say enough about what they have done with the place. It is currently home to more than a hundred happy aircraft.

Wayland and I were initially introduced to Dwayne on the phone during our dinner at the cafe. Larry knew one of the field's tenants who happened to stop by our table and I inquired about services for the Fleet. "Here," he said, handing me his cellphone. "Talk to Dwayne; he'll fix you right up."

"No problem," said Dwayne. "Get some gas and oil right there at the restaurant and then push your airplane over to that open hangar with the Beechjets in it. It can stay in there for the night."

I wasn't even going to inquire about the availability of hangar space. That's usually a luxury item when you're barnstorming across the country.

"Then," he continued, "just walk across the runway to my house. We're having a pool party. You guys can stay in the downstairs guest rooms."

I wasn't even going to inquire about the availability of guest rooms.

After promising to keep in touch, we said goodbye to Larry, serviced the Fleet, and an hour later I was being pulled across Dwayne and Julie's backyard swimming pool by a golf cart with a ski rope attached. Yes, alcohol was the culprit but, remember, the flying was done for the day and the airplane was put to bed for the night. Before we had crossed the runway from the hangar where we'd parked the Fleet, I had called Dwayne to make sure it was okay to just walk across the runway without asking anyone's permission. I have had my butt chewed more than once for assuming it was allowed, even after looking both ways.

Dwayne chuckled and said, "Don't worry. It's fine. The only rule here is to just use some common sense."

I nearly dropped my phone. There actually exists an airpark populated with airplane people who conduct their flying activities with, dare I say it, common sense as a guideline? It cannot be! Wayland, the Fleet, and I must have flown through some cosmic prairie portal after we left Beaumont. Yes, that has to be it! We were somehow transported to a Neverland airport where common sense and good judgment have not yet been supplanted by litigiousness and the fear of liability. Well, praise the Lord and pass the Bud Light! I hope that portal stays closed behind us.

We passed an absolutely idyllic airport evening by the pool. Way across the runway I could still see my yellow Fleet sitting among the business jets in the hangar. It looked like a scruffy stray hound in the company of well-groomed show dogs, but that was okay with me; I had a traveling airplane, slow or not. It was streaked with engine oil and I'd be doing some more dope and fabric repairs when I returned home, but it has never left me stranded. And let's face it, it's not the kind of flying machine in which just anyone would enjoy traipsing around the country. It has no GPS, no VOR, and no electrical system whatsoever except for the battery which powers the radio and intercom. It's just needle, ball, and alcohol, as the old timers used to say.

It was late in the evening when all of Dwayne and Julie's flying neighbors retreated to their own airport homes and hangars scattered along the runway. Wayland and I were pretty beat as a rewarding day with many newfound friends came to a close. I had been trying to explain to him since our trip began what airport folks could be like and I think he was starting to get the picture. It's a difficult phenomenon to describe, especially to someone not used to being around airports and airplane people. It has to be experienced firsthand to be truly appreciated.

Complete strangers had just opened up their home to us, sight unseen and without hesitation, because we all share a love of the blue.

# CHAPTER THIRTEEN

WE WOKE UP AND showered while it was still dark outside, although the sun would be coming up soon. The early morning sky showed signs of being another clear, hot flying day. Dwayne had coffee ready upstairs in their main kitchen, so Wayland and I walked up and sat around the bar listening to more of his and Julie's history. They'd met when he was a factory test pilot for Beechcraft and she was a new hire, as well as his apprentice. Inevitably, since there's no better way of getting to know someone than in an airplane cockpit, they were married. In addition to owning and operating Stearman Field, they fly and manage several corporate jets, all as an encore to their test pilot careers with

Beechcraft. Which is where their oldest son, only in his mid-twenties, is currently a test pilot. This is a flying family if ever there was one.

After cooking us a scrumptious breakfast at his restaurant before customers began to arrive, Dwayne drove us to the hangar where we had parked the Fleet. We preflighted and prepared for another day of wandering around the Midwest. Our first destination, and the genesis for our journey, would be Greensburg. None of us who had cooked pigs for the town in the aftermath of the devastating tornado had returned since. So it had become mine and Wayland's three thousand-dollar cheeseburger.

The morning air was still and cool when we lifted off Stearman Field and flew north a few miles before turning west in order to avoid the innermost airspace surrounding the Mid-Continent Airport in Wichita. The outside air temperature was perfect for open-cockpit comfort and the visibility was almost unlimited; there was the slightest perception of haze just above the ground.

Just underneath Wichita's Class C airspace at a thousand feet above the ground, we crossed the Arkansas River within a mile or two of four giant towers looking down at us. Then we angled southwest toward Cheney Reservoir which we could see in the distance. This heading would take us to the town of Kingman, which sat right on Highway 54, and that highway would take us straight to Greensburg.

We had called another friend, Matt, who lived in Greensburg, before departing Stearman Field. He was going to meet us wherever we could land as near to Greensburg as possible, although he'd told us the old grass strip in town was now closed. Somehow it didn't survive the reconstruction of the town after the tornado, which was disappointing to hear as well as a bit confusing. Why would a town willingly forfeit its only airfield? No doubt politics had raised its ugly head somehow and therefore there could be a hundred reasons why it had happened. We would deal with landing options after we arrived; we would have two hours of fuel once we were overhead the town and could easily backtrack to other airports if necessary. In fact, there were two regional airports between Wichita and Greensburg, one at Kingman and one at Pratt.

It was relaxing to be able to navigate on this first leg of the day without having to constantly consult a chart on my lap that flapped in the wind. And, not being as young as I used to be, I'm constantly putting my reading glasses on and taking them off in order to read the chart. So following the highway to our destination allowed me to enjoy the morning's flight and to look around a bit. Now, some people will argue that there isn't much to see when flying across Kansas, but I disagree. The Midwest is a hauntingly wide open space that triggers the imagination, especially from our viewpoint a thousand feet in the air. I always think of the westward migration a hundred and fifty years before.

What an adventure that must have been for all those folks leaving the East in search of something better. And Lord knows what the Native Americans thought about it, doomed as they were. My mind always wanders back to the same question: Why wasn't everybody able to just stay out of each other's way? To live and let live? Obviously that's a naïve notion on my part, but when I fly across such a vast land as the United States, even at only a thousand feet above the ground, I can't help but wonder why there wasn't plenty of room for everybody to do their own thing. I mean, the prairie just seems to go on forever. But I guess sooner or later everyone wants to use the same watering hole, and, voila, you've got a conflict.

There was also a railroad track that ran beside the highway we were following, but there were no trains this morning. I wanted to find a train rolling along out in the open so I could wave to the engineer in the locomotive. It's just something I've always wanted to do. Actually, there were quite a few man-made structures in what was seemingly the middle of nowhere. We saw several fish hatcheries, a couple of small gas wells, the ubiquitous grain silos, and an occasional farm house. How quiet and peaceful it must be to grow up in this kind of rural atmosphere. Teenagers no doubt would vehemently disagree, but at my age, I think of what a good night's sleep you could get way out here on the prairie.

About ten miles east of Greensburg there was a grass strip that sat beside a service station on the south side of the highway. It would be a good alternate at which to meet our friend, Matt, if we couldn't find a good landing spot any closer, so we flew on. The first thing we noticed from the air about Greensburg as it came into view was that it had obviously been cleaned up since we were here last. We had seen the town about a month after all the terrible destruction and it had looked like old photos of World War One battlefields with rubble strewn everywhere among the twisted remains of trees.

Now though, it was as if someone had begun a whole new town, which in essence they had. The new, modern buildings stood out in the center of town and scattered about in what were once full neighborhoods were the new homes. The empty lots where nothing had been rebuilt were conspicuous. We could see the grove of cottonwoods on the east side of town that had survived the tornado and was where we had held the Fourth of July celebration five years before.

The old grass airfield was indeed no longer in use and was bordered on one side by a new housing development as well as bisected by a wide ditch. But in spite of that, there was still room for us to land and, more importantly, take off again. I circled several times to assure myself of where all the pertinent obstacles were located. My main concern was the aforementioned ditch and some power lines at the approach end of the now-shortened field. But we slipped down over the wires and touched down softly on the dry grass with plenty of room to spare after rolling to a stop at the north end.

Our friend, Matt, was standing by his truck just across the ditch as I shut down the engine and we unstrapped ourselves; he'd been watching us as we circled and landed. He looked the same as we remembered as he walked over to shake our hands. He and this whole community had been through many trials since we saw them last. In truth, they had persevered and emerged as a model of how a town can bounce back from such an awful tragedy. A world model, as it turns out. They had written a new chapter on how to rebuild better and stronger than before and were now the example many cities all over the globe looked to for inspiration and guidance. And Matt had been a large part of all that. He is also the inventor and purveyor of delicious Duck Salt seasoning, an exquisite addition to any kitchen's spice rack.

I admire the townspeoples' fortitude, but I think if I'd been in their shoes I would have said the heck with it. If a big-ass tornado blew everything I owned clear to the North Pole I think I'd just put the insurance money in the bank and start walking down the road and never look back. But, of course, I'm speaking from absolutely zero experience with such a traumatic event, thank goodness. Obviously the people of Greensburg loved their town and never considered not rebuilding it.

We spent the rest of the morning touring the new and improved LEED-certified town. The design and planning that had gone into the now more tornado-proof, self-sustaining community was impressive. The city hall, the hospital, and the high school were exemplars of green, environmentally-friendly construction and engineering, and it was clear that the townspeople who had returned were very proud. Some of them remembered us from when we had come to cook for them that sad summer and some did not, but of course it had not been about us, so that was okay. It was all very heartwarming to see what had been accomplished in the past five years. I'm still in awe.

Around noon it was time to leave. We were bound for Iowa and wanted to make some progress in that direction while high pressure areas still dominated most of the Midwest. Matt drove us back to the temporarily operating runway and as we were getting out of his pickup I could see that the Fleet had attracted some admirers. They were mainly curious why someone had landed where there wasn't supposed to be an airfield any longer. We said hello and explained our presence while we looked over the Fleet.

One astute gentleman asked if we would be able to take off okay. He was reading my mind because, as most pilots know, it's usually easier getting into a landing area than getting out of it. And of course the wind was not blowing from the direction I would have preferred. It was still slightly favoring the direction in which we had landed which had been fine for landing but, as the strip had a bit of a slope, I wanted to take off downhill, opposite the direction we had landed. Finally, I decided that departing uphill and into the wind was best, since the obstacles were identical on each end of the field, basically telephone pole-height power lines. I knew the Fleet would get off the ground quickly so I wasn't too concerned, and then we'd be climbing into the wind.

My rough performance calculations were accurate and we were a hundred feet in the air above Matt's head as we crossed the wide ditch where the Fleet had been parked. We could see everyone below us waving. We waved back as we circled the field once and then pointed our trusty flying machine northeast.

# CHAPTER FOURTEEN

A TEN-MINUTE FLIGHT PUT us over the small regional airport just north of the town of Pratt; it was the last municipal airport we had flown over on our way to Greensburg earlier that morning. And best of all, it was open for business. We hoped that since our return trip home would not coincide with any holidays, we would have less trouble finding airports with FBOs operating on their normal schedules.

It was almost lunchtime when we'd left Greensburg, but we had wanted to get in the air so we had skipped eating and now we were hungry. So while we enjoyed vending machine snacks and a soda, I pieced together my collection of charts and soon realized that they did not quite reach all the way into southeastern Iowa where we were headed. The elderly gentleman who operated the FBO had none for sale that covered the areas I was missing, but he did have some out-of-date ones that would. I slid these around on the floor of the office until they overlapped in such a way that I could see the big picture of where we were trying to go. Usually a large wall chart is ideal for this sort of flight planning but there wasn't one, so I made do.

Eventually I could see what our general heading towards Blakesburg, Iowa, needed to be, factoring in an occasional deviation one way or another in order to avoid busy airspace and restricted areas. Even though we can only go a hundred and twenty to a hundred and eighty miles on each leg depending on the winds aloft, I like to have the big picture in my mind before setting off. So, with a full tank of gas, plenty of oil, and a new heading to hold, we said goodbye to the folks at the Pratt Airport and began our journey back to the Tarheel State via Iowa.

The area of northern Kansas we were navigating toward had lots of airports to choose from once we reached the two-hour mark, so I was withholding my decision as to exactly where we would stop next. In the meantime, we both enjoyed the scenery of the Kansas prairie as it passed below us. We flew over the occasional power line and railroad track which stretched across the lonely flatlands and there was even a small river every now and then. But it was lonely, barren country until we approached Hutchinson, the first sizeable town we'd actually seen since leaving Wichita.

We flew around the northwest side of the city, crossing the Arkansas River for the second time on our journey, to avoid Hutchinson Municipal's airport traffic area. It had been a little over an hour since departing from the airport at Pratt, so I started thinking about where we might stop next for gas and oil. At that point, we had only traveled about seventy-five miles so we had a slight headwind and I realized we would not go as far as I had hoped on our two-hour leg.

It really should not have been a problem except that I got us lost. Again.

Oh, I don't know how it happened. I knew generally that Interstate 70 was fifteen or twenty miles north of us and that Wichita was about forty miles south of us, but I just could not determine our exact position. This of course makes it hard to determine the correct heading to the airport I had decided on for our next fuel stop. Each little railroad track and stock tank combination started looking like all the others and the first thing I knew, I was completely befuddled.

I didn't want to wander into Salina's airspace or the nearby Restricted Area and I didn't want to wander too near Ft. Riley either, which had an even larger Restricted Area, so I kept hunting and pecking more eastward, hoping to get my bearings. Somehow I had managed to be smack dab in the middle of nothing, where there were no discernible landmarks. It didn't help to be only a thousand feet above the ground where it's more difficult to spot towns and lakes in the distance, but I so hate to waste fuel by climbing higher, which in the Fleet is agonizingly tedious. Finally we spotted the small northwestern tip of Lake Marion and after flying due east for about twenty minutes we crossed a big highway running north and south. That put us almost exactly in between the airport I wanted to go to and the smaller one near the town of Marion. I chose the bigger one, well, because it looked bigger on the chart.

Herington Regional Airport, roughly between the towns of Herington and Council Grove, looked like an old military airfield with its three dilapidated concrete runways forming an odd triangle. Actually, only two of the runways were dilapidated and they were both marked with giant yellow Xs, warning us that they weren't useable. The third one though was useable so we touched down and taxied to what appeared to be the ramp, stopping beside the self-service gas pump. Our theory that most FBOs would be open now that Memorial Day had passed did not seem valid because there was a small airport office building but there was nobody inside. There was however air-conditioning as well as both a vending machine and a drink machine which would provide us with another delicious meal. First things first though and we went outside in the scorching afternoon heat to service the Fleet.

Wayland added a couple quarts of oil as I prepared the pump and hose for fueling. We were done in twenty minutes and we went back inside to savor the luxurious coolness of the little airport building. I spread our charts out on a big table in the middle of the main room and roughly calculated our next stop. It looked like we might be spending the night in Missouri, assuming of course that I didn't get us lost again.

This next leg would carry us about halfway of the remaining distance to our destination in Iowa. But there would be a bit of a dogleg in our route since I wanted to stay well clear of the huge Kansas City Class B airspace. We would also need to cover around a hundred and twenty miles before we would start having some good choices so far as airports with services were concerned. Although we hated to leave the relative comfort of the little airport building, it was soon time to climb back in the Fleet and resume our journey.

# CHAPTER FIFTEEN

AS WE CLIMBED TO the northeast of Herington Regional we could see that the topography was finally changing; we started to see some small hills below us. They only rose a hundred feet or so above the flats, but it was definitely different from the severely flat prairieland of central Kansas. For the first thirty or forty miles we were roughly paralleling a railroad track, but it finally turned more eastward and left us. Off our left wing in the distance I could see the buildup that was Ft. Riley and its surrounding towns.

Soon we crossed the Kansas River near a small town called St. Marys and off our right wing was Topeka and just beyond was the urban sprawl of Kansas City. It was almost fifty miles away but we could still make out the tallest buildings. At that point we'd been flying about an hour and it looked as if we would easily make it over into Missouri with plenty of fuel to spare.

For a while after crossing the river, we flew along without any major landmarks. There was the occasional small township usually intersected by two roads which were also the section lines and there were tiny lakes sparsely scattered about. Many of the little communities had distinctly Native American names such as Powhattan, Hiawatha, and Huron. Of course, the names made me wonder how those places came to be named as they were. To my knowledge, those were all names of tribes from the eastern United States, not the Midwest. I made a mental note to investigate the towns' origins when I returned home.

Eventually we were approaching the Missouri River and the state of Missouri. Actually, we crossed the Missouri exactly at a spot where three states converge and where there also happened to be a small island situated in midstream. This was quite unintentional on my part but we left Kansas, briefly stuck our toe in Nebraska, and entered Missouri while covering less than half a mile across the ground. The Missouri is quite a historically significant river as much as its famous cousin, the Mississippi. A little more than two hundred years ago, President Jefferson had tasked Lewis and Clark, along with their hardy band of woodsmen, to find a route to the Pacific Ocean. They had spent a large part of their trip on the Missouri River, from St. Louis to the wilds of what is now Montana. Now that had been an adventure!

We were a little less than thirty miles from what appeared to be a good airport at which to stop for the evening. The land in northwestern Missouri was much greener than that from where we had come; the rolling hills of wheat and corn seemed much more lush than farther west. It was always enchanting to watch the world below change over the course of just one day's travels in a slow old biplane. A former college professor of mine used to say that whenever he drove across the United States with his family on vacation, he was always reminded of the lyrics of *God Bless America*. I can honestly say that impression is multiplied by a hundred when flying low over America in an open-cockpit biplane. You can smell the land beneath you. The fresh-mown hayfields, the stockyards, the forests of cedar and pine, the salt air, and much more.

Northwest Missouri Regional Airport soon came into view sitting on a rise just west of the quaint college town of Maryville. It was surrounded by gently rolling hills of tall grass and there was even another airplane in the traffic pattern, which was something we had not seen much of on our journey thus far. From the air, the town promised to have all the amenities for a relaxing evening as we could see several shopping malls and ample motels and restaurants, always welcome sights.

After joining the traffic pattern behind the other airplane, we landed and taxied to the ramp in front of the FBO and shut down near their fuel pumps. Every place has a different feel when you land and first take stock of your new surroundings and this airport had a friendly, down-home feel to it. It was also obvious that we were no longer in the more arid, hardscrabble portion of the Great Plains; this countryside was more eastern than western in that everything was green and well-irrigated. It reminded us more of our home in the South than western Kansas had.

The husband and wife managers of the FBO were very hospitable and arranged for a rental car after we paid for our gas and oil. Then we pushed the Fleet across the ramp to a tie-down spot near the edge of the concrete and wiped off the day's oil and grease from around the engine and the front cockpit before putting the covers on. Then I put the gust lock on the rudder and we tied it down nice and snug. It was ready for its second night outside since we had left home three days earlier, which wasn't bad since you never know whether or not you're going to have hangar space when you land somewhere unannounced. But the weather promised to be good in Missouri for the rest of the week so I wasn't too worried.

Our first order of business was to find our way into town and secure ourselves two rooms for the evening. It was a pleasant drive from the airport and quite scenic. There were more trees than we had seen since leaving Wichita and the whole countryside was filled with thriving cropland. It was a little cooler too, though not by much. We passed the college on the edge of town which appeared to have some ongoing summer classes based on the number of students we saw on campus, and we soon found ourselves on the main street of Maryville.

It is always anticlimactic, not to mention extremely restful, to be out of the Fleet after a long day of flying and navigating. Not that I don't enjoy every minute of it, but it is mentally and physically draining especially in one hundred-degree weather. It always makes me think what hardy souls those early aviators were in their open-cockpit machines who, unlike us, didn't have an air-conditioned motel room and a cold beer waiting for them at the end of the day. They must have loved to fly.

Eventually we chose a Holiday Inn Express that seemed suitable and there was a Mexican restaurant we'd seen en route to the hotel which we intended to visit for dinner. In an hour we both had showered and put on clothes relatively free of oil and grease and were sitting in the La Bonita with a frosty pitcher of Dos Equis and homemade chips and salsa in front of us. Words cannot adequately describe the contentedness I feel at times like that at the end of a successful day of piloting. I was sporting a clean pair of underwear and sitting down to a wonderful meal with a good friend; it simply does not get any better than that.

# CHAPTER SIXTEEN

WE WENT TO BED early and woke up to clear skies and much cooler temperatures than we were used to so far on our trip. The town of Maryville was just beginning to stir as we drove back down the main street toward the airport. It was going to be a lovely morning to resume our flight to Iowa. The Fleet was where we had left it and all its surfaces sparkled with dew. After returning our rental car and saying good morning to the folks at the FBO, we began our ritual of preparing for another day's flying.

It was time to grease my rocker arm shafts again so I began while Wayland packed up our cockpit and engine covers and stowed our small overnight bags in their proper places. By this time we were becoming expert at working as a team prior to getting airborne. The Fleet is neither a large nor a complicated airplane, but there are nevertheless a certain number of tasks that cannot be overlooked when you are barnstorming far and wide. The trick is to take your time and not be in a hurry to get in the air, which practice also lends itself to savoring the moment.

Our trusty flying machine practically leapt into the cool Missouri morning. Fortunately we had each put on a lightweight fleece pullover in anticipation of the temperatures at a thousand feet. On all our previous mornings it would be eighty degrees by the time we took off, but not today. This morning was just right as we waved a last goodbye to the FBO folks and took up a northeasterly heading towards Blakesburg. We passed over downtown Maryville as its inhabitants were beginning another day and then we were over the picturesque landscape of northwest Missouri.

There was more of everything below us now; more power lines, more houses, more small townships, and more water than we saw when we had been farther west. Near the little town of Parnell we crossed the Platte River which led south towards the bigger Missouri. Then came the Grand River which was pointed toward the Missouri as well. Our destination this morning was Antique Airfield near Blakesburg, Iowa. Much like the Beaumont Hotel, it was an airport I had wanted to visit for many years.

It has been the home of the Antique Aircraft Association for almost sixty years and, much like the Experimental Aircraft Association in Oshkosh, is a place where like-minded airplane people have been carrying the flame of grassroots aviation for a long time. It is different than its more sophisticated relative in Wisconsin though. Somehow, in spite of its longevity and popularity, it is still just a downhome grass airport in the middle of the Iowa farmland, without pretense or apology.

We reached our halfway mark right over the town of Lamoni, which sat beside Interstate 69 that ran north to Des Moines and south to Kansas City. It also meant we were in Iowa. I immediately started looking for the town of Winterset on my chart; it suddenly dawned on me that we could go see the birthplace of John Wayne. Unfortunately, it was almost fifty miles out of our way and I scolded myself for not thinking of it earlier. It was also the area whose covered bridges were made famous by Robert James Waller's enchanting love story.

I didn't dare tell Wayland about Winterset over the intercom; he would have mutinied. Detouring to see the world's largest stuffed prairie dog or some other extravagant gaudiness is what keeps him going. I was thankful he didn't have his own chart in the front cockpit, or worse, a Triple A roadmap with all the tourist traps advertised on it. Some things are best kept from the crew. So we happily motored on, watching the tranquil Iowa landscape below us. There were quite a few small rivers and creeks, all of which seemed to be tributaries of the Missouri River farther to the south.

Before long we could see Rathbun Lake over our nose, which meant we were almost to Blakesburg. Again I found myself both fascinated and curious about the names of several little towns we flew over. There was Mystic, just up the road from Brazil, and Iconium, just across the lake from Confidence and Bethlehem. What great names those were. And just beyond Iconium was the intersection of two railroad tracks, one of which slowly bent around to the east and would lead us straight to our destination.

The tiny hamlet of Blakesburg sat right where it should have and we flew a couple of circles above it to look it over. A few pickup trucks were moving about the streets and the town seemed to be awake on such a fine morning. I assumed they were used to seeing an antique biplane overhead considering the proximity of Antique Airfield, but who knows. We continued following the railroad track three or four miles northeast of town and there we found the two intersecting grass runways and all the hangars which are the Antique Aircraft Association.

After flying over the field to see how things were laid out, we entered a left downwind for the north-south runway. There were no other airplanes in sight, on the ground or in the sky, but it was the middle of the week so that was not too surprising, even here. The wide grass runway slopes up from both ends toward the center and as soon as we touched down my motor cut off. I had no idea why it cut off but we still had lots of momentum and were able to coast all the way to the parking area in front of the hangar that housed the museum.

"Do you always shut it off for landing?" asked Ben, the grandson of the airfield's patriarch, who had been watching our approach. I assured him I did not and that I wasn't sure why it had done that, although I suspected it had been idling too slowly after I'd pulled back the power to land.

The airfield was indeed a nostalgic place with its two grass runways which intersected near an assembly of old-style hangars and outbuildings where several big trees provided ample shade. A nice lady in the airfield's office made us a fresh pot of coffee, as we were still a little chilled by the morning's flight from Missouri. After we had warmed up a bit, Ben gave us a grand tour of the grounds starting with the Air Power Museum.

I would not have suspected such an eclectic variety of aircraft and engines and memorabilia was in the nondescript metal building which housed the museum. They even had two Fleets in their collection. And next door there was an extensive aviation library with some impressive first editions. This was a place I knew I would return to when I had lots more time on my hands. They have for more than half a century been hosting an annual fly-in around Labor Day weekend that lasts five days and I promised myself I would bring the Fleet back to attend one of these soirees as soon as I was able.

I never cease to be amazed at what a small world it is, especially in aviation, and, sure enough, Ben and I had both worked for the same firebomber company out in Wyoming many years before. It had not been at the same time and he had been a mechanic and I a co-pilot but we had known the same people. That's what I love about the flying business; no matter where you land, someone always asks if you know so-and-so who flew this or that for whomever. And, in most cases, you do in fact know that person, even if not very well.

Soon it was time to continue on our way so we took a couple of photos beside the Fleet, added some engine oil, and then got it cranked. I wanted to do an engine run-up to satisfy myself there was nothing out of the ordinary going on with the magnetos or the carburetor. If it did need some technical attention, I was in as good a place as any for advice and assistance regarding an antique Kinner engine. As soon as it was warmed up I pointed it into the wind and performed a magneto check and all indications were as they should be; it idled properly too, so we taxied back to the south end of the bigger runway for take-off.

We were only going over to the regional airport ten or twelve miles away in nearby Ottumwa for fuel. The skies were still as clear as a bell with unlimited visibility as we broke ground abeam of the museum right where the runway crested. I climbed straight ahead to gain a few hundred feet of altitude and then turned left two hundred and seventy degrees so I could make a low pass down the crossing runway. Skimming along the grass, we waved to Ben as we went by.

I was secretly envious of him as I climbed up for a better view of the countryside in order to get my bearings over to Ottumwa. Of course I have no idea how he feels about it, but I imagined how wonderful it must have been to grow up at Antique Airfield. It would be like the little kid at Willy Wonka's chocolate factory or like the son Hugh Hefner never had, growing up at the Playboy mansion. Okay, that's probably not a good analogy but you get my point.

Ben was the third generation of the family that has helped guide and sustain the momentum of the association for more than half a century; his granddad is one of the original members from the old days. I was sorry we had not had the opportunity to meet him, as I'd heard he was quite the character. Can you imagine growing up around all that airplane stuff and then for some reason not being interested in learning to fly? That would make for some awkward moments around the dinner table.

I would definitely return to Blakesburg. It is Shangri-la for antique airplane people, which according to Webster's dictionary means "a remote, beautiful, imaginary place where life approaches perfection." I could not have said it better myself.

# CHAPTER SEVENTEEN

FOR ME, THE REST of our trip could take whatever shape it chose; I had accomplished all that I had intended on this adventure by having visited the Beaumont Hotel and Antique Airfield; everything else would be icing on the cake. We'd had some unexpectedly pleasant experiences in Wichita and had seen our old friends from Greensburg, but from now on we had no specific plans in mind. We would just leisurely make our way back home to North Carolina.

But first we needed to fill our tank with avgas and our motor with oil so we looked for the regional airport just outside the city of Ottumwa. We could see that the Des Moines

River pretty much bisected the town off to our right as we passed to the northwest. Then we spotted the airport and were perfectly lined up to land on Runway 04, so we continued our long final approach.

Ottumwa Regional had a big, spacious ramp as well as a big, spacious FBO. We shut down in front of the main office building and the fuel truck came to us. After filling the Fleet with 100LL and stowing extra quarts of engine oil for our next leg, we went inside to pay. I cannot say that I have ever met rude folks who manage an FBO, they depend on return customers after all, but let's face it, some are more personable than others. And the folks at Ottumwa are some of the friendliest and most helpful I have ever done business with. They asked if we knew of Antique Airfield, a logical question considering the vintage of our conveyance. We told them we had indeed just left there and were now on our way home but had every intention of returning in the near future.

We extracted a quick lunch and refreshment from their vending machines and retrieved our charts from my cockpit in order to calculate our next general area of landing. It looked like we would easily make it to Illinois on our next leg and navigation would be a breeze since we would be following the Des Moines River southeast all the way to the Mississippi. And of course the farther east we went there were more and more airports to choose from for our next fuel stop, which would be somewhere just north of St. Louis.

After starting the Kinner, we strapped in and taxied down to the end of Runway 31 to depart to the northwest. After breaking ground we banked left in the clear, early afternoon sky and turned toward the city of Ottumwa and overflew downtown as we pointed our nose southeast to follow the river.

We had had nothing but gorgeous weather for our entire trip and, except for the heat and humidity, we had no complaints whatsoever. And this afternoon was no exception as we motored along above the scenic farms of Iowa. We stayed just northeast of the river, watching it flow along below our right wing. There was one tiny township after another established along its banks with people and cars moving through the neatly laid-out streets. Was Libertyville full of free-thinkers? Was Keosauqua an old Native American village? Did they wear stylish socks in Argyle? Was Bonaparte founded by Frenchmen? That's what I thought about as we passed contentedly above those small towns in America's breadbasket.

In fifty-some miles we once again came upon the mighty Mississippi River into which the river we were following emptied. Here the Big Muddy formed the western border of Illinois where a few days before and a little farther south we had barely stuck our toe for a couple of hours while looking for fuel. Today, though, we had the opportunity to fly right across the heart of the Land of Lincoln. Just forty miles downriver was Hannibal, Missouri, and Tom Sawyer's famous whitewashed fence. But we did not detour for that famous landmark of folklore either and instead continued southeast, enjoying the sights and smells of the central Illinois farms. We were also passing through some large MOAs so I was keeping a vigilant eye on the skies around us in case the military was training today, but we never saw anything in the air besides ourselves. Technically, we were flying just beneath the floor of the training area at a thousand feet above the ground, but when it comes to fast-moving fighter jets, you can't be too vigilant.

In a while we saw the Illinois River in front of us, signaling that we were approaching our two-hour mark. This river too flowed into the Mississippi but originated far to our north out of Lake Michigan and meandered through the giant metropolis of Chicago before spilling onto the rural Illinois countryside. It also meant we were almost beyond the Military Operations Areas we had been flying near.

The Jacksonville Municipal Airport was easy to find. It sat in the middle of the flat farm fields and pastures which surrounded the town of Jacksonville. The town sat right beside Interstate

72 which ran east and west across the state. Our heading had us on a long, straight-in final approach to Runway 13 but there was another airplane in the traffic pattern so we entered the downwind for a landing behind it. This was only the second time on our trip we had encountered other airplanes in the pattern when we were landing. It's always fun to watch another aircraft maneuver in the pattern, touch down, and take off again. I always feel an instant camaraderie with whoever is in the cockpit.

The airport seemed to have been an old military airfield. It didn't have the typical three runways forming a triangle but it did have some large, unused concrete pads and aprons that definitely weren't for civilian use. And the whole complex was sprawling and spacious, an indication that Uncle Sam had designed it years ago. When it was our turn to land, the five thousand-foot runway appeared to go on into infinity as we touched down on the wide span of asphalt. It seemed to swallow up the Fleet as we taxied toward the FBO at the far end of the runway.

The little Piper was still in the pattern shooting touch-and-gos when we came to a stop in front of the gas pumps. I am always optimistic when I see flight training in progress; at least one more person in the general population is learning to fly. And I always secretly hope that they finish what they started and do not get discouraged or run out of money before they at least get their Private Pilot's license. I think sometimes we pilots take the need to fly for granted. Each of us takes his or her own form of enjoyment from flying of course, and hardly any pilot takes that aspect of it for granted, but what fascinates me is that there are actually people who have no desire to learn to fly.

How can someone live in a civilization where flying machines of all shapes and sizes exist in abundance and not have the desire to learn to fly them? I learned to fly helicopters simply because I could not stand the thought of there being a type of aircraft I did not know how to control. So, I think sometimes we pilots don't realize that we have an innate need to operate machines that go up in the air. To perform an act which we wish we could perform naturally but instead have to depend on a machine. But that is okay, we accept that dependence. At least we can still leave the ground, albeit with an aircraft attached to us.

In all fairness to my non-pilot friends, they probably wonder why I do not fish or hunt or play golf. My love of flying is most likely as much a mystery to them as their lack of interest in flying is to me. They are most likely thankful they have not been beset by whatever has attracted me to these darn contraptions. But, really, how can someone look up at a blue sky full of puffy white clouds and not want to go up there and scoop up part of it in their hand?

We unfolded ourselves from our cockpits and stretched our legs a bit before beginning our servicing of the Fleet. The slight breeze blowing across the concrete, which was quickly warming up, felt good in the afternoon heat. We were already envious of the cool morning temperatures we had enjoyed earlier in Maryville. After fueling from the self-service pumps, we walked down the ramp to the FBO office to see if they had engine oil for sale and to flight plan our next leg.

Greatly relieved to find that they indeed had the oil we needed, we lingered as long as we could in the air-conditioned lobby, scouting for vending machines. Wayland paid for our oil while I bought our lunch which consisted of Lance crackers and cold sodas in the can. While we enjoyed our meal, which we had come to think of as our pre-take-off snack, I drew a line on our charts to see what lay approximately two hours farther southeast. It looked as if we would get as far as Indiana and maybe even into Kentucky before dark. We'd been enjoying a slight tailwind since leaving Ottumwa and therefore a slightly higher groundspeed. I hoped that would continue to be the case.

With our fuel bill settled and our appetites satisfied, we walked back down to the Fleet to begin our next leg. As we climbed into our seats I saw the little Piper turn off the runway onto the taxiway and head toward the FBO. It looked like they were done with their flight lesson for the time being. We waved to them as they went by us and I silently wished that student pilot the best of luck in getting his license.

# CHAPTER EIGHTEEN

THE FLEET CLIMBED ANXIOUSLY to the southeast out of Jacksonville as we pushed on. Even though we were still four or five states from home, depending on the accuracy of my navigation, we were starting to smell the barn. Having met all of our goals in visiting friends and historical sites, we were starting to get a little homesick.

I have always thought I would like to spend an entire summer touring around the United States on the Fleet, taking my time to drop in on whatever airfield seemed inviting or had some ongoing celebration or pancake breakfast. But every time I actually take an extended cross-country trip, I realize that I might not actually want to be gone from home that long. The First Great Fleet Biplane Excursion was mine and my wife's trip to the Grand Canyon and back home across the Rockies from North Carolina; but we split that into two trips due to our work schedules, taking the airlines home after getting to Arizona and then back again on the airlines to retrieve the Fleet two weeks later to resume our trip.

Maybe that's the sensible way to do it. Or maybe one day I'll try that grand tour, but for now, we just have to get back across the Appalachian Mountains to North Carolina. By the end of the day we would be close.

It wasn't long before we could see the city of Springfield, Illinois, off our left wing about twenty miles in the distance. The visibility was great and the taller buildings stood out clearly. The land was still fairly flat but became more and more populated the farther east we went. There were also many more private airstrips denoted on my chart as well, another indication that we were leaving the West and the less populated counties. Our route would occasionally take us directly over a private airstrip and I always circled above it to see what was there.

Sometimes it was just a crop duster's strip with a T-hangar and a concrete ramp area for loading their chemicals and maybe one or two ag planes sitting around. And sometimes it was a nicely manicured turf runway beside a private home with a beautiful metal hangar and well-kept grounds on lots of acreage. Those were always my favorite. If there were people outside they would look up and wave as if they were waiting to see if we were going to drop in and say hello or, often in my case, ask for directions. I think it would be very rewarding to visit all those private airfields and meet all those airplane people.

I recently had a pilot friend of mine ask me if he can land unannounced at the little airports marked as private airfields on the sectionals. He is a very experienced pilot and has flown all over the world but has not done much grassroots VFR flying in the United States. I told him that indeed you can and what's more you would most likely be very welcome and even invited to stay for dinner and spend the night. At least that has always been my experience.

Yes, I know some of the urban legends involving little innocuous airfields in the middle of nowhere which are in fact clandestine government facilities are true, but they are extremely rare. And even if you innocently stumbled upon one and landed, you would just be politely invited to depart immediately. You would not be vaporized by a death ray and never heard from again. Or so I've heard.

If you think about it, it is a rare airplane person who builds a grass strip for himself or herself, along with a home, and then doesn't want anyone to drop in for a visit. Sure, some pilots are grumpy old misanthropes, but they are as rare as those clandestine government airfields. Most airplane people love to meet other airplane people and to hear about where they've flown in from and where they are going. Not to mention the fact that we love to look at each other's airplanes.

I have always had a theory that states if you drive onto someone's property on a motorcycle and ask to pitch a tent and spend the night, you may or may not be granted permission, but if you land at someone's airstrip and ask to spend the night, you will always be allowed. So far this theory has held true for me no matter where I have gone in the Fleet in the United States. Although there was that one time when I wore out my welcome and the lovely siren I was visiting at a high, mountain strip in Colorado couldn't wait for me to leave. I like to think I'm more mature now, but I'm probably not a good judge of that. Anyway, I am digressing and none of that has anything to do with my original theory.

Fifty miles off our right wing was the sprawling city of St. Louis, once one of the few meccas of all things aviation in America between the world wars. It was the stopping place whenever airplanes were attempting their transcontinental, record-breaking flights, as well as one of the earliest hubs for transcontinental airline service, complete with some of the first air traffic controllers. And, most famously, it was the home field for the Lone Eagle when he was just a mail pilot and not yet an international celebrity.

If I could travel back in time to the 1920's, the Lambert St. Louis Flying Field, as it was then called, is one of the aviation sites I would want to visit. Just to sit at the counter of the little airport diner as the pilots of Mr. Robertson's air mail service, including the lanky, twenty-one year-old Lindbergh, came in to eat after a mail run to Chicago and back would be highly enlightening. Nostalgia is definitely a driving force for those of us who are enamored with antique airplanes and in spite of our appreciation for the advance of technologies like GPS and ADS-B, we long for the early days of flying and what we perceive, probably wrongly in some cases, as a simpler time.

On we went, enjoying the smooth afternoon flight across Illinois, where for quite a while we did not see much of anything. There were not even many tiny townships for twenty or thirty miles, but we did notice that the land below us was starting to roll and become hilly. And we could see more and more creeks and rivers as well; the land was green and well-irrigated.

We were still enjoying a tailwind of about fifteen miles-per-hour and it looked as if we would travel two hundred miles on this leg, which was something we were not used to. At a glance, I estimated we would certainly be in Indiana and almost back in Kentucky at our next fuel stop.

After crossing over the Kaskaskia River, we soon came upon the northeast and southwest-bound traffic of Interstate 70, speeding along between St. Louis and points north. And, for once, our groundspeed was greater than the vehicles on the highway beneath us. We started to see more lakes too, all of which were fed by the now abundant streams. One creek, called the Little Wabash, ran near the community of Bible Grove. No Sunday School shirkers in that place, I bet. I imagined a big revival tent and long tables stacked with home-cooking after an uplifting sermon by a firebrand of a country preacher. Looking down though, I didn't see a church. Maybe it was over in the next little community of Sailor Springs; surely one would be needed there.

Two hours into our flight we were across the bigger Wabash River and into Indiana thanks to the wind on our tail. The Wabash ran into the Ohio where the states of Illinois, Indiana, and Kentucky all meet near the town of Unionville, but that was off our right wing to the south. We could however see the city of Evansville, Indiana, in the clear air; it sat right on the Indiana side of the slow-moving Ohio River just north of where we had crossed the river on our way to Kansas.

I had chosen the Huntingburg Airport as our fuel stop and, sure enough, we had traveled just over two hundred miles, which was another first for us on our trip. We rarely covered more than a hundred and fifty miles on our way west on each leg, so our blazing groundspeed this time had been a nice treat. The uncontrolled airport was located a few miles south of the town of the same name and just north of the interstate highway.

We touched down on the long east-west runway and followed the FBO's directions over the radio to their self-service fuel pump which was located several hangars away from the airport office building. It was late afternoon when we landed and it was our fourth leg of the day, counting the short hop from Antique Airfield over to Ottumwa. We were making good progress thanks to our consistent tailwind near the surface and had logged almost six hours of flying since we left Maryville, Missouri. The day had not been a scorcher like the ones we'd experienced while en route to Kansas, so we weren't nearly as tired as usual. In fact, after we fueled the Fleet and added some oil, we decided to fly one more leg before stopping for the evening.

We spread our charts on top of the metal cabinet which housed the fuel pump and took a gander at what lay ahead of us in the general direction of home. If our tailwind continued we would cross over into Kentucky and be very close to Tennessee after going another two hundred miles. I considered New Tazewell in north-central Tennessee as a potential destination but that would push the limits of my comfort with reserve fuel in the Fleet, not to mention the FAA's legal limits. It would all depend on our thus far accommodating tailwind so we decided to head in the general direction of New Tazewell and reserved the right to alter our flight plan as we went.

Since we had not made time on our way to Kansas to visit my friends in Tennessee, I thought I'd make an attempt on our return. It had been several years since I had been stranded at their airport due to inclement weather and I really wanted to see them again. During my stay that week, they had treated me like a newfound member of their family and had extended to me and the Fleet every hospitality. They had graciously driven me down to Knoxville to catch an airline flight after I reluctantly left my airplane in their hangar. It was the only way I was able to make it to the airshow in Slayton, Texas, on time, which had been my goal in the Fleet.

We folded our charts and stowed our odds and ends of flight gear back into our two cockpits and prepared for our last flight of the day.

# CHAPTER NINETEEN

AS IS SO OFTEN the case, this would be our most enjoyable leg of the day. The sun was getting low in the western sky and was no longer boring down upon us and nor was it in our eyes. It was at our backs and the temperatures were cooling down as we climbed away from Huntingburg. The sky was also still clear with not a cloud to be seen.

The terrain below was starting to change significantly too. We were approaching the foothills of the Appalachian Mountain chain and there were noticeable swells in the land which ran northeast and southwest. It was very picturesque and it reminded me again how fortunate we are in America to have such a vast, changing landscape from sea to shining sea, not to mention the freedom to access practically all of it, even by air.

The first landmark to catch our eye after departing to the east was the Castle on the Hill, a majestic brick and stone monastery that stands sentinel over the town of Ferdinand. The architectural masterpiece is crowned by a huge Romanesque dome and stands over a hundred feet in the air. We had a spectacular view of the grounds and I wondered if the Benedictine women monks who lived there had ever had the opportunity to see their home from our perspective. I would dearly love to have given them all a ride in the Fleet. Every time I have given a person of the cloth an airplane ride, especially in an open-cockpit, they inevitably analyze it from some heavenly perspective. Of course, I couldn't agree with them more. Although, *heavenly* isn't the word I would use to describe the times when I'm standing on my head trying to safety wire a hard-to-reach bolt with safety wire pliers in one hand and a mirror in the other and terrible expletives are issuing forth from my mouth. I'm digressing again.

We circled the Monastery Immaculate Conception a couple of times and then continued southeast toward Kentucky. Just past the monastery we crossed Interstate 64 and were soon passing over a rural area of farms and pastures, all gently rolling toward the Ohio River which formed the southern border of Indiana. The odor of grass and plowed dirt was mixed with the pungent exhaust of the Kinner. The lovely river town of Louisville was nearly forty miles away and slightly ahead of our left wing, but we would be nowhere near its Class C airspace as we crossed into Kentucky.

When we were twenty-five miles from Huntingburg I checked my watch to see how long we'd been flying in order to determine our groundspeed. It was a little less than on our previous leg, but I expected that to be the case since the winds often die down late in the day. I realized that we might not make it all the way to New Tazewell after all, but there were plenty of airports we could choose from if we had to pick a new destination.

Northern Kentucky was no less scenic than the southern part of the state had been earlier in the week. We flew just to the south of the Restricted Area around Ft. Knox, enjoying the vistas of lush farms irrigated by an abundance of small creeks. It was becoming noticeably more mountainous too; the terrain was rising into long, narrow razorback ridges beneath us and I had to climb the Fleet a few hundred feet to stay a thousand feet above it all.

We were constantly pointing out to each other the stately homes built on the sides of some of the ridges. What a wonderful view those folks must have every morning when they go out on their deck for a cup of coffee. Not as great as our view of course, but on the other hand, much more convenient.

After flying for an hour, we had covered almost ninety miles but it would still be cutting it close to make it to the New Tazewell Airport in Tennessee. We motored on as I made some more calculations with my handy E6B whiz wheel computer. If our tailwind continued we could make it to our destination with exactly thirty minutes of fuel remaining, which made it a legal proposition. But add to that the fact that we'd be arriving late in the day with long shadows being cast in the foothills, my unfamiliarity with the area, and therefore the very real possibility of getting lost just before dark in a day/VFR-only airplane, and I decided discretion was the better part of valor.

So somewhere above the little crossroads hill town of Clementsville, Kentucky, and just east of Green River Lake, we changed our course to more easterly and headed toward the two towns of London and Corbin. There was a municipal airport situated between the towns that we assumed would have everything we needed for the Fleet and most certainly everything we needed for a comfortable night's stay. And all I had to do was navigate well enough to cross Interstate 75 and then follow it to the airport.

There was an ulterior motive to our landing at the London-Corbin Airport. As a bit of trivia that only Wayland would be aware of, London, Kentucky, was the home of Colonel Sander's first Kentucky Fried Chicken restaurant, established in the 1940's. They even host each year the Annual World Chicken Festival, which, much to Wayland's chagrin, we would miss.

It was indeed almost sundown when we saw the interstate in front of us and I knew we had made the right decision by not flying deeper into the Clinch Mountains where New Tazewell was situated. The last thing I wanted to be doing in the Fleet was stumbling around at near dark in the mountains with only reserve fuel trying to pinpoint a small airport. My dad and I never flew together much after I started flying for hire, but one thing he told me when I was learning to fly which I have never forgot is to never be in too big of a hurry to get to where I was going. Some pilots call it *get home-itis*, a deadly syndrome which has killed many aviators who were not willing to divert to a different destination or, for that matter, to cancel a flight altogether when circumstances dictated that they should have.

You cannot go through life without being scared to death from time to time, but I do my best to avoid being scared out of my wits in an aircraft of any kind. I am a lover of the blue but I prefer to limit soiling my britches to when my feet are planted firmly on the ground. It's easier to find a restroom and a clean pair of underwear that way.

I love the old aviation pearl of wisdom which states that good judgment comes from experience and, unfortunately, experience comes from bad judgment. I suppose the trick is to have survived all the times we exercised bad judgment and to somehow learn from them. I never stop learning whenever I fly but, being human, I still make mistakes. I like to think though that nowadays my mistakes are no longer the kind which could have the catastrophic consequences of the mistakes I made when I was a younger, more inexperienced pilot. Only time will tell, I suppose.

For me, aging gracefully as a pilot means to continue learning about aircraft, maintenance, weather, regulations, technology, and much more, but with the additional advantage of all the cumulative experience and wisdom I have gained thus far. The other thing my dad once told me which I have never forgot is that whenever I think I have an airplane mastered, I had better stop and rethink my overconfidence because I'm most likely getting ready to really screw up. That sage advice always pops into my mind whenever I tell myself what a great landing I just made.

We touched down at the London-Corbin Airport and taxied to the spacious general aviation ramp in front of their FBO, shutting down in a freshly painted parking space complete with new tie-down rings. Man, was I tired. It had been our longest day of flying so far on our trip at almost eight hours of flying time, including four fuel stops, which are labor-intensive affairs with an antique biplane. All in all, it had been nearly a twelve-hour day of continuous flying, servicing, and flight planning and we were both a little fatigued as well as a little wind burned.

After deciding to delay fueling and oiling the Fleet until the next morning due to our lack of energy, we extracted our overnight bags from their respective cockpits and began tying down the airplane and securing its covers. The Fleet had been performing flawlessly for us all week and I discreetly patted its cowling and thanked it for a heretofore wonderful journey, promising it some tender loving care when we got home. Wayland probably wasn't ready to hear me talking to my airplane just yet; I didn't want to erode his confidence in me after already getting us lost twice. And the trip wasn't over.

Adjacent to the FBO was an airport restaurant with a patio facing the ramp. It was happy hour so it was full of revelers, most of whom had pitchers of beer on their tables, none of which went unnoticed by me and Wayland. We considered going straight to the restaurant and joining them but decided we needed to shower first and change into some clean clothes before our second public debut in Kentucky.

The FBO graciously loaned us their crew car and gave us directions toward London where they assured us we could find suitable lodging. We drove north toward London from the airport and within a few miles we did indeed find a nice hotel and got ourselves checked in and cleaned up. Within a half hour or so we met in the lobby and received further driving instructions from the helpful lady at the front desk who directed us to the Shiloh Steak House, just a couple miles up the road. She guaranteed us we would find good food and an assortment of cold beers.

It was already dark outside as we sat and enjoyed our meal, completely exhausted by the day's travels but completely satisfied by what we considered a home-cooked meal compared to what we normally found in all the FBO vending machines. We had flown a long way since leaving Maryville, Missouri, earlier that morning and had covered more than seven hundred miles and crossed four states.

In these modern times of smartphones and privatized space travel, I can see why that doesn't sound like much of an accomplishment, but it makes me realize how wondrous airplanes must have seemed to people when the first practical flying machines were developed. Before the First World War, when the first students from both the Wrights' and Glenn Curtiss's flight schools were unleashed upon the doubting American public, imagine the boundless amazement of everyone who saw them perform at the early airshows and flying exhibitions. Even though automobiles and telephones were already being used at the time, it still must have boggled their minds to see men and women negotiating those invisible currents of wind with the greatest of ease in their heavier-than-air machines.

Altitude and endurance records were made and broken almost on a daily basis. The criteria for each new record-breaking flight were constantly changing to keep up with the constant advancements in both powerplants and aerodynamics. While those advancements were not at the pace we would see during the upcoming four horrible years of world war, they were significant nevertheless. The newspaper-reading public must have wondered where it would all end. Could those daredevil maniacs and their flying machines just keep going up and up until they were in the heavens? Was there no end to the possibilities? They could not have been any less astounded than we are today by the rapid advance of our current technologies.

In the early Eighties I was a firebomber co-pilot for a colorful captain named Andy, who once introduced me to his then ninety-something-year-old grandmother who was still spry and sharp as a tack. She lived alone in a quiet neighborhood in Denver, Colorado, and had come out west in a covered wagon with her family in 1905 as a young girl. That was the same year the Wright brothers were flying around Mr. Huffman's pasture outside of Dayton in their much-improved 1905 Flyer. It could carry two people, both sitting upright, and take off from level ground. Imagine what Andy's grandmother would have thought if she had looked up and seen that Wright Flyer pass overhead as she and her family were trudging across the Great Plains in their wagon. What a contradiction that would have seemed like. A brief convergence of our past and our future.

Wayland and I philosophized into the evening on these very ideas as we enjoyed our dessert followed by coffee, eventually making our way back to our hotel for a much needed night's sleep.

# CHAPTER TWENTY

WELL-RESTED AND WELL-FED AT the hotel's free continental breakfast the next morning, we hoped the day's flying would see us back home in North Carolina. The morning was cool at sixty-five degrees as we pulled into the courtesy car's parking space in front of the FBO and the sky promised another clear, blue flying day. We had a bit of servicing to do before we could depart, so after turning in our car keys and requesting the fuel truck, we walked out to uncover the Fleet. After stowing our overnight bags in their usual places, Wayland began the uncovering ritual while I began the rocker box greasing ritual. The grease was noticeably more viscous in the cool morning temperature but I eventually completed my task without having to refill my grease gun, which is always a messy affair. Right on cue, the fuel truck arrived just as we were done.

I topped off our tank with 100LL from atop the fuel guy's step ladder and then I added three quarts of oil. It was Wayland's turn to pay for gas so he headed back to the FBO office with his credit card. I thanked the fuel truck driver and gave the Fleet a good looking over while waiting for Wayland to return. Preflight inspections should always be thorough and never rushed, but I took even more time than usual this morning, not wanting to overlook anything on this last day of our travels. Wayland soon walked back across the ramp and assumed his now-familiar position in the front cockpit.

Soon the Kinner was idling happily with the sun shining right on its cylinders as it appeared ever so slowly over the airport terminal building. After a ten-minute warm-up, we taxied to the hold line for a southerly take-off. The magnetos showed a tolerable drop in RPMs and all indications looked normal on the engine gauges. I added power and we started rolling and were off the ground in the crisp, cool air very quickly and climbed over the interstate and turned left toward the hills. The air was so still I could sense immediately it was going to be one of those glassy smooth mornings for flying, even over the mountains. We would have to cross Pine Mountain first as we headed southeast away from London across the Daniel Boone National Forest.

I was wearing my fleece jacket and the outside air temperature was absolutely perfect for a comfortable morning flight. We'd had the foresight on the ground to don warmer clothing since the Fleet cockpits are not roomy enough for a two hundred-pound pilot to easily add or remove clothes in-flight. Not to mention the fact that the biplane does not fly hands-off very well either. I could see that Wayland was thoroughly enjoying the spectacular views of the fog-shrouded valleys. It's interesting how you can know what the person in the front cockpit is feeling about the flight, or how you can know what they're about to say to you on the intercom. The ridgelines were protruding through the low clouds like islands and even looking straight down I could not see the ground below us.

There was nothing but clear blue above us but as far as I could see in front of us there were only more valleys covered in fog. It was a fantastic sight and not something you get to enjoy every day, even in an old antique biplane, but for peace of mind I wanted to know how widespread the fog was versus what the forecast had said. From experience I knew the poor visibility close to the ground would become worse as the sun rose higher but then the hot summer sun, with no cloud layers between it and the fog, would burn everything away eventually. But, if you're not planning for the worst case scenario, you're not planning very well.

So I started tuning in some of the automated weather reports from the airports along our route. One-quarter and fog, one-eighth and fog… whoops. We had another hour and a half of flying before we were down to my personal comfort level of landing with one hour of reserve fuel onboard. By then I knew we would be well across the mountains and all the fog would be gone to wherever it goes when the sun chases it away. Based on that logic, I was feeling better about my weather decision. Even though nothing happens too quickly in a seventy-five mile-per-hour biplane, it doesn't mean you can't screw up.

The other minor consideration was where to land if the engine quit. The best places down in the valleys were all obscured by a hundred-foot-thick fog bank, which left us with tree-covered ridges. Not great, but better than having only options which involved zero visibility. Besides, sometimes you have to have more than the usual amount of faith in the engine that is turning your propeller. I have always said that an airplane does not know over what type of terrain it is flying, or whether it is day or night, but sometimes I wonder. If the Kinner does indeed know, I hoped it would not have a warped sense of humor and decide to screw with me by running slightly roughly, or by letting its cylinder head temperature creep up ten degrees and scare the bejeezus out of me.

And it didn't. After thirty minutes of heavenly views of mountain ridges surrounded by thick white blankets you could walk on, the fog became thin and wispy. The valley below us was flat and wide and the towns showed themselves from underneath. We were only a mile north of a little paved municipal airport which sat beside the Powell River in far western Virginia and we had passed just north of the fabled Cumberland Gap of Daniel Boone fame, but had not actually seen it due to the fog. Once we crossed the wide valley we were in Tennessee and had flown through three states in about an hour and would soon be in North Carolina.

Faith in my flying machine or not, I'd be lying if I said I didn't breathe a sigh of relief once we were beyond all those parallel ridges of Pine Mountain. We still had to negotiate the majestic Blue Ridge in front of us but I was certain I could find the pass through it which I had not been able to find on the first day of our journey.

I turned more to the south so we would remain well below the floor of the Terminal Radar Service Area which was more than thirty miles in diameter and encompassed all three of the cities which made up eastern Tennessee's Tri-City area. The innermost portion of the airspace surrounded the regional airport, which was roughly equidistant from Bristol, Kingsport, and Johnson City. As we skirted Kingsport to the southwest and turned back east toward Johnson City, we could see the early morning traffic on the maze of multi-lane highways below us. Just east of Johnson City, the smaller town of Elizabethton pointed us to the western edge of Watagua Lake, which would lead us to the pass over the Blue Ridge and on to flatter land.

The skies were still clear and smooth as we passed over the lake and we could see the pleasure boats sliding around on the surface. I steered the Fleet along the long finger of water that pointed toward a low place in the high ridge ahead of us. We were seven or eight hundred feet above the ground as we left the lake which then became a river that snaked through the canyon. A two-lane highway ran beside the river and we followed it to the college town of Boone. We were back in our home state then.

It was the middle of the morning and the main street of Boone was busy below us. I wondered if anyone was looking up to see what manner of contraption was making its way up their lovely mountain valley. We flew right over the little private airport in town where one lonely metal airplane was tied down beside the runway. There was no activity there this morning. What a shame, because it was an exhilarating morning to be in the sky, to cross a mountain, to fly over a lake, to thread through a canyon, and to be back home.

Having diverged from the river, the highway was soon by itself as we left Boone behind us and the road meandered down the mountainside to the southeast. We kept following it as the ground dropped away beneath us and we could start seeing farther into the distance where the land was opening up. It would get flatter and lower as we flew east, eventually meeting the Atlantic Ocean at sea level hundreds of miles away on the far side of the state. Navigating would be relatively easy from here on since Interstate 40 bisected the entire state of North Carolina and led almost exactly to the rest of our stops.

We would have to make one more fuel stop before our last leg back into Air Harbor where Wayland would be leaving me and the Fleet. The Wilkes County Airport was directly in our path along Interstate 40 just north of the town of Wilkesboro and was the perfect place to land. Flying above the relatively flat land east of the Blue Ridge Mountains was completely stress-free for me. Those of us from the coastal plains of North Carolina consider Wilkes County to be in the foothills but, regarding survivable emergency landing sites compared to what we had passed over after leaving London, it was relatively flat. So I was mentally relaxed as I enjoyed the last day of our adventure.

# CHAPTER TWENTY-ONE

THERE WAS NO LOCAL airplane traffic to be heard on the Unicom frequency at the Wilkes County Airport as I reported our position when we were ten miles to the west and announced that we were inbound for landing. It was a quiet, peaceful morning at their airport as we turned a left base for Runway 01 and landed to the north. This was our first landing in our home state since leaving for Kansas five days earlier and we were happy to be back. There really is no place like home.

No sooner than we had taxied to a stop in a parking space in front of the FBO, an elderly gentleman was making his way toward us. He had come from a nearby hangar and had a big smile on his face but I didn't recognize him as someone I knew. I shut off the Kinner and was climbing out of the rear cockpit as he approached.

"I thought I heard a Kinner in the distance," he said. "What model Fleet is that?"

That's usually not the first thing I hear from most bystanders. Most folks think my airplane is a Stearman when they see the Fleet from a distance and then they realize it's something else as they get a closer look. But every now and then there's a Kinner man in the crowd and that's what Robert Phillips was. He had two Kinner-powered Ryan trainers in his hangar which he invited us to see and we gladly accepted. One was a pristine restoration in flying condition and the other was awaiting a new Al Ball-overhauled engine. Robert was a fellow lover of the blue and an antique airplane aficionado; I hoped our paths would cross again soon.

Wayland and I thanked him for the hangar tour and said goodbye before walking back to the FBO to request service from their fuel truck.

Soon we had the Fleet full of avgas and oil and idling happily down the taxiway for departure. There still wasn't any traffic in the pattern so we turned onto the active runway and departed to the north. We banked to the right and climbed above the rolling hills and could see forever in every direction. This would be Wayland's last leg of his first open-cockpit biplane excursion and I wondered what he was feeling. I also hoped he had enjoyed himself, although I was pretty sure he had. If you stop and think about it, a ride around the patch in an antique airplane is one thing, but to volunteer for the equivalent of a transcontinental flight is something else altogether. But Wayland never wavered and, truth be known, he had been much more relaxed than me overall, especially when we were negotiating the mountainous portions of our routes.

In fact, he had already suggested some obscure destinations for our next adventure, whenever that might be. We had discussed going back out to Blakesburg for their annual event or maybe even all the way to Wyoming to visit some friends there. Crossing one mountain range would no longer satisfy Wayland I suppose; now he was determined to make me and the Fleet cross two of them. I should have been flattered by his confidence in both me and my airplane. Or perhaps he only wanted to test the limits of my nerves.

We crossed the Yadkin River just east of the airport and would be paralleling it and the interstate almost all the way to Winston-Salem. It was only an hour's flight to Air Harbor and Wayland had called his wife, Jane, before we departed Wilkes County to give her our ETA. We were in no great hurry to complete this last leg of our trip and were both luxuriating in the warm mid-morning sun and the smooth air. The sky was a deep blue and still showed no signs of the inevitable haze of late May. It wasn't long before we could see the proud, prominent knob of Pilot Mountain to the north off our left wing and soon after that we could make out the tallest of the buildings in downtown Winston.

I turned about ten degrees more to the north to make sure we were well clear of the Smith-Reynolds Airport's traffic area and after a few more miles we crossed the Yadkin River a second time as it turned to the right and meandered down to High Rock Lake thirty miles south of us. Winston-Salem was behind our right wing as we flew over the little town of Walnut Cove and then turned back to the east. It wasn't long before we were over Belews Lake which was roughly at the edge of Greensboro's Class C airspace. At a thousand feet above the ground we were just below the floor of the outer ring and I angled the Fleet a little southeast towards the tiny Air Harbor airpark which was still ten miles away. We flew just to the right of a two thousand-foot tower which stared down at us off our left wing. I shook my head wondering what stalwart soul had to climb to its top to service the antennas and lights. That chore would not be for the faint of heart and I for one could never do it, not even for all the beer in Milwaukee.

About five miles out I gave a position report on Air Harbor's frequency and listened for other traffic but didn't hear any. Wayland and I began searching for the airfield but it is always difficult to spot from a low altitude. It's nestled among tall trees and surrounded by the rural suburbia of northern Greensboro so that it blends in very well with its surroundings. But the small, irregularly shaped lakes nearby always help me pinpoint the runway and eventually I recognized the opening in the woods which was Air Harbor and we circled overhead to check everything out.

It looked just as we had left it a week earlier so we entered a left downwind and turned final to the east, touching down on the grass to the right of the narrow asphalt runway. I taxied the Fleet to a stop in our old parking space on the grass right in front of the barn hangar with the yellow Taylorcraft in it and shut down the motor. We were back at our starting point safe and sound. I sat in my cockpit for a few moments not really wanting to get out. It had been another perfect morning for flying and I wished it had been a longer leg. I was of course glad we were back although I had a couple hundred more miles to go to get to my home field, but mine and Wayland's journey as a crew was over.

Jane soon arrived and walked down to say hello while Wayland gathered up his odds and ends of gear from the airplane and I put on the rudder gust lock and tied down the wings. We were suddenly starving and decided on lunch at Fisher's Bar and Grill in downtown Greensboro, our favorite local watering hole. As we walked up the hill to the gravel parking lot near the tiny airport office, I turned around to look at the Fleet. It was the only open-cockpit biplane in the entire tie-down area, which was full of the usual assortment of high- and low-wing metal airplanes, and it proudly sported streaks of engine oil down its fuselage and rocker box grease on its windscreens. It seemed to be sitting patiently while I allowed it to rest for an hour or so.

Sitting at Fisher's and eating one of their delicious sandwiches in celebration of our completed biplane trip was anticlimactic for me and Wayland. Our adventure was over. There was no vending machine food to eat for lunch and no new destination to plot on our chart. And no need to service the Fleet in the hot summer sun. And worse, I couldn't offer a toast in the form of a cold draft beer because I had more flying to do to get home. So, we mostly ate in silence, occasionally answering Jane's questions about our trip. We promised each other to come up with another reason to venture across the country in the Fleet as soon as possible.

After we had eaten, Jane and Wayland drove me back out to Air Harbor and helped me untie the wings and then they stood by the tail while I cranked the motor to life. The Fleet and I lifted off the asphalt easily and I banked around to fly down the runway and waved goodbye to Jane and Wayland, who were standing beside their car in the gravel parking lot.

# CHAPTER TWENTY-TWO

I WAS ALONE WITH my airplane for the first time in more than thirty hours of flying. It's always a special time when it's just me and the Fleet. I looked it over thoroughly from my rear cockpit as we flew along. The yellow duct tape I had applied in Missouri to part of the trailing edge of the top wing was still in place. And the slight fuel seepage around my sight gauge I'd first noticed in Kentucky was still there. And most importantly, the Kinner was clacking along nicely with no unusual sounds or vibrations.

I love this little airplane. I am often behind the learning curve in its upkeep but I am always trying my best to do right by it and it always rewards me with a memorable flight like the one this morning. All those moving metal pieces and parts, humming like my mama's old Singer, never out of sorts with each other, and only a minute's quiet glide from certain damage should an emergency landing be necessary. I am so proud of it. I wondered if any of its peers were up in the air this fine pilot's day, having crossed a mountain range just after sunrise, returning home from halfway across America? Most likely there were not any. Most likely they were safe in their snug hangars and maybe, just maybe, they'll go around the patch late in the evening if it's not too windy. My Fleet is a traveling airplane; it's no showpiece. That's what I tell people when they see its cosmetic blemishes up close. Mr. Simpson would be proud of his airplane.

The sun was directly above as we headed east away from Greensboro and the downtown skyscrapers off the right wing were clearly visible. The land was much flatter now but not completely so and we were over farms and pastures immediately after departing Air Harbor. We were back in a part of the country where landmarks were familiar to me and I didn't need charts to find my way home. That is a comfortable, relaxing feeling and is always a bit of a relief when on a long cross-country flight. To be almost home and your charts could escape over the side of the cockpit but it wouldn't matter because there is that big crooked lake and there are those ridiculously tall towers and there is the big power plant whose smoke stacks are beacons.

We crossed the Haw River north of the town of Burlington and I could see all the traffic moving east and west on the interstate a few miles to the south. Over the radio I could hear a couple of airplanes working in the traffic pattern at the Burlington Airport but they were too far away to see. On we flew taking in all of the sights and smells familiar to us as we got closer and closer to our home field.

But first I wanted to land at Ball Field northeast of Louisburg to say hello to some friends I've known for more than thirty years. The airfield was founded by its namesake, the redoubtable Joe Ball, a local flying legend and purveyor of all things Stearman. Joe has gone West but his tomb stands a quiet vigil over the runway. He and the Ball Field gang were pilots I looked up to and aspired to emulate when I was a brand new commercial pilot a long time ago, and I still do. I was immediately drawn to the grassroots atmosphere and camaraderie of their airport the first time I visited and I knew way back then that it was my kind of airfield. Joe's nephew, Vernon, now lives beside the airport and I never come and go on any Fleet excursion without stopping at Ball Field. It would be like driving through Memphis without going to Graceland.

We continued beside the interstate until downtown Durham came into view which meant we were halfway to Louisburg. I could see the clearing within the urban buildup of Chapel Hill that was the Horace Williams Airport. I steered the Fleet slightly more north to avoid the upcoming Class C airspace surrounding Raleigh-Durham International and we crossed a four-lane highway on the northern edge of

Durham where the scattering of lakes of the greater Falls Lake was visible ahead of us.

It was only Thursday but the lakes had several boats pulling water skiers and most of the picnic areas along the shores held quite a few people and cars. We dropped down a few hundred feet to wave to them and some of them waved back. Little did they know we were returning home from a round trip to Kansas via Iowa and the Great Plains. But how could they? We climbed back up to our previous altitude and I took in the familiar countryside below me. The freshly plowed and planted fields were surrounded by tall pines and two-lane back roads and every now and then we flew over a meticulously manicured horse farm trimmed with bright white fences. I saw one farmer on a huge red tractor with a lanky, multi-armed implement in tow and I waved to him but I was too high for him to see my gesture.

It's so relaxing not having to study a chart while you fly. You have so much more time to enjoy the scenery passing by under your wings.

And at times like that I fantasize about never having to land and never needing to refuel; just flying on and on forever until I have seen everything there is to see from the air. I expect those same thoughts went through the minds of early aviators who wanted to go farther and faster and higher in their rudimentary machines.

I began looking for U.S. 1 up ahead and then I would know if I was on course or not. If the town of Franklinton was off my right wing, then I was on course and, if not, I would adjust accordingly. The little town was just where I hoped it would be so I started looking for the blue water tower and soon spotted it. Then the town of Louisburg appeared over the nose of the Fleet and I pointed us a little more north until I saw the big, open field with the pond and right beside that was Ball Field.

I circled over Vern's house several times before he finally came outside and headed down to the airfield in his golf cart. By the time I touched down on the grass beside the narrow, paved runway, he was parked by the clubhouse waiting for me. The clubhouse is a veritable museum of old aviation photographs and mementos of more than fifty years of flying exploits by the Ball Field gang. The still photos which cover the walls belie the colorful, eccentric personalities though. I'm surprised someone has not written a book about the history of this airfield but they are probably waiting for the statute of limitations to expire on some of the more disputable occurrences.

"Are you coming or going?" asked Vern.

I told him where we had been and he just shook his head. I had stopped here on the Fleet when returning from the Rocky Mountains one summer, so he wasn't really surprised. But I could tell he thought it was a substantial accomplishment in the Fleet and that made me feel good. He offered me a cold beer, which he had in abundance in the cooler strapped to the rear of his golf cart, but I declined and told him I wanted to land over at Sky King Ranch before flying on home.

We talked for a while longer and then he propped the Kinner for me and I taxied to the north end of the paved runway and took off. I banked the Fleet around and flew over the roof of the clubhouse as Vern looked on, then I gave Joe a salute and climbed back up to some slightly cooler air and started looking for the tall antenna that always helps guide me to Sky King Ranch.

# CHAPTER TWENTY-THREE

MY LONG-TIME FRIENDS, STEVE and Diane, live at Sky King Ranch, a picturesque eighty-acre property complete with livestock pastures, a big fish pond with its own white sand beach, and, of course, the turf runway. Thirty years ago I had flown the jump plane that deposited Steve and his best man, Mark, into Steve and Diane's outdoor wedding. They have always been one of my favorite aviation couples. Diane is a professional flight attendant by trade and the epitome of the down-home country girl with Southern good looks and the sassiness to go with it. Steve has flown everything from crop dusters to 747s and his call sign as a U.S. Marine Corps fighter pilot was *Hostile*, which pretty much sums up his gruff exterior, but actually hides a more compassionate side, to which several stray dogs can attest.

My favorite photo of them together is one where Steve was the captain on a round-motored Douglas DC-3 and Diane was the stewardess. They are standing in front of the number one engine below the high flight deck and they look like Ken and Barbie in their nicely tailored uniforms. The photo could have been from the 1940's if you didn't know better.

The doors to the Quonset-style hangar were open so I knew they were home even though I had not spotted them from the air yet. After checking the condition of the grass airstrip, I slipped down through the gap in the tall pines at the south approach end and touched down right on the end. Steve's runway requires a slightly unorthodox base-to-final turn and really is not for the novice pilot. Nor is it perfectly level as there are several humps which rejoice in sending you skyward again if you have landed with too much airspeed. The Fleet though had lived in their hangar for five years alongside Steve's Skybolt, so we were not unaccustomed to the requisite landing technique.

I parked on top of the slight rise in front of the hangar and shut off my engine just as I saw Steve walking toward us and Diane was coming from the other direction in her golf cart with their dog, Shasta, a sweet animal shelter rescue, in the front seat beside her. Stopping here to visit is always a respite from life's travails. It's so quiet and peaceful and the hospitality is always warm and sincere, just as a place like this should be. Any pilot would be lucky to get stranded at Sky King Ranch on their way to anywhere.

We retired to their back porch which overlooked the back half of the ranch. The freshly mown pasture sloped away from their house down to the small lake and we sat in the shade enjoying iced tea as I told them a little about our trip. Steve entertained the idea of flying his Skybolt to Blakesburg if I decided to go the next year in the Fleet. I wanted to spend the night and visit longer but I needed to get back to Todd's Cross before dark.

I borrowed five gallons of avgas from Steve so I would have a comfortable reserve en route to my home field, which would be the last leg of the entire journey. The extra gas would keep me from having to make another fuel stop before reaching home. I added some engine oil and then strapped into my cockpit, saying goodbye to Diane and Shasta while Steve prepared to give my propeller a whirl.

We S-turned down the narrow runway to the south end and spun around to get lined up for take-off. The Fleet bounced along on the grass, becoming airborne prematurely once or twice before we were solidly flying. After climbing over the power line at the north end of the airfield and banking around to the left for a low pass over the hangar, I waved to the three of them as the Fleet and I climbed away to the east.

Our journey was almost over. In about an hour's flying time we would be back at our home field. The skies were still fairly clear although a little hazier than earlier in the morning. And it was still smooth above the flat farm fields and the pine tree plantations. The land was becoming noticeably flatter as we continued east. I saw the big X formed by the two gigantic power lines which crossed one another and told me my compass heading was correct so far. I watched the spark plug wires vibrating in the slipstream in front of me and marveled at the reliability of the Kinner. By the time we get home we will have logged almost forty hours of trouble-free flying.

We crossed Interstate 95 just a few miles north of Rocky Mount and I could see the high school in the distance off my right wing where I took my Private Pilot check ride in the late Seventies. The high school wasn't there back then of course but has since been built on top of the site of the old downtown airport. For a number of years you could still recognize from the air where the old runway used to be, but no more. It's sad when an airport goes away, regardless of the reason. It had been one of the airports my dad's dad used to drive his whole family to on Sunday afternoons. And my grandfather was not even a pilot.

Once we were beyond Rocky Mount, I was officially in eastern North Carolina. There were fields of young tobacco plants everywhere and I could almost smell hickory-smoked pork barbecue on the wind. The land was definitely flat now and would remain that way all the way to the Atlantic Ocean. The town of Tarboro was a few miles to the south as we continued eastward and I soon saw the break in the trees ahead of us that was the Roanoke River. We crossed the river directly over the two-lane bridge where the blacktop road led northeast out of the quaint little town of Oak City.

We only had to cross a ten-mile wide dark forest of a swamp which makes up the Roanoke River low ground before we would be within sight of Windsor, my hometown. The southwestern portion of Bertie County is a vast, heavily-forested swampland of cypress trees and old-growth hardwoods. I could see some of the taller giants sticking up above all the others. To me, flying over this kind of terrain, even though it's flat, is just as hazardous as flying across mountains. If I had to land the Fleet down in that Roanoke River low ground, we might not be found for a while and I would be on the wrong end of the food chain if I tried to walk out. But, of course, the Kinner chugged along smoothly without even a hiccup to scare the bejeezus out of me.

Soon we were safely across and the thick timberland became scattered farm fields again and I could see the town of Windsor in front of us. We circled the historic downtown area once and then over to mama's house on the southeast edge of town to let her know I was back from Kansas. I pointed the Fleet toward Old Highway 17 and followed it out of town to the northeast. It was only five miles as the crow flies to Todd's Cross Airport where the Fleet and I live. The tall yellow tank on top of which sits my windsock soon came into view. We circled the field to check for deer and standing water but there were none of those things so we approached from the east over the tall pines and touched down softly on the grass which had grown quite a bit during my absence.

I shut down the motor in front of my hangar and sat there taking in the sounds and smells of my airplane as it started cooling down. My face was sunburned and my eyes were wind burned but it had been another fun-filled, rewarding excursion in the Fleet. It could have a much deserved rest in its dry, snug hangar now. I had tried to explain to Wayland several times during our trip how those Stearman guys wouldn't be caught dead in an antique like the Fleet. Hand-propping the engine at every stop and greasing rocker arms once a day becomes a tedious chore very quickly if you're just a weekend antique airplane pilot. But if you have a barnstormer's soul you consider the oil on your clothes and the grease under your fingernails to be a badge of honor.

That's your airplane on your hands and it knows it. Airplanes have souls and that's why I talk to the Fleet. Try crossing the wooded ridges of Pine Mountain in Kentucky with a solid layer of fog beneath you without talking to your airplane. Can't be done.